Regulation and Compliance in Operations

Butterworth-Heinemann – The Securities Institute

A publishing partnership

About The Securities Institute
Formed in 1992 with the support of the Bank of England, the London Stock Exchange, the Financial Services Authority, LIFFE and other leading financial organizations, the Securities Institute is the professional body for practitioners working in securities, investment management, corporate finance, derivatives and related businesses. Their purpose is to set and maintain professional standards through membership, qualifications, training and continuing learning and publications. The Institute promotes excellence in matters of integrity, ethics and competence.

About the series
Butterworth-Heinemann is pleased to be the official **Publishing Partner** of the Securities Institute with the development of professional level books for: Brokers/Traders; Actuaries; Consultants; Asset Managers; Regulators; Central Bankers; Treasury Officials; Compliance Officers; Legal Departments; Corporate Treasurers; Operations Managers; Portfolio Managers; Investment Bankers; Hedge Fund Managers; Investment Managers; Analysts and Internal Auditors, in the areas of: Portfolio Management; Advanced Investment Management; Investment Management Models; Financial Analysis; Risk Analysis and Management; Capital Markets; Bonds; Gilts; Swaps; Repos; Futures; Options; Foreign Exchange; Treasury Operations.

Series titles

- **Professional Reference Series**
  The Bond and Money Markets: *Strategy, Trading, Analysis*

- **Global Capital Markets Series**
  The REPO Handbook
  The Gilt-Edged Market
  Foreign Exchange and Money Markets: *theory, practice and risk management*
  IPOs and Equity Offerings
  European Securities Markets Infrastructure
  Best Execution in the Integrated Securities Market

- **Operations Management Series**
  Clearing, Settlement and Custody
  Controls, Procedures and Risk
  Relationship and Resource Management in Operations
  Managing Technology in the Operations Function
  Regulation and Compliance in Operations
  Understanding the Markets

For more information
For more information on **The Securities Institute** please visit their Web site:

www.securities-institute.org.uk

and for details of all **Butterworth-Heinemann Finance** titles please visit Butterworth-Heinemann:
www.bh.com

Regulation and Compliance in Operations

David Loader

ELSEVIER
BUTTERWORTH
HEINEMANN

AMSTERDAM BOSTON HEIDELBERG LONDON NEW YORK
OXFORD PARIS SAN DIEGO SAN FRANCISCO SINGAPORE
SYDNEY TOKYO

Elsevier/Butterworth-Heinemann
Linacre House, Jordan Hill, Oxford OX2 8DP
200 Wheeler Road, Burlington, MA 01803

First published 2004

British Library Cataloguing in Publication Data
Loader, David
Regulation & compliance in operations – (Securities Institute. Global capital markets series)
1. Business enterprises – Finance 2. Industrial management
3. Compliance auditing
I. Title II. Securities Institute
658.1′2

ISBN 0 7506 5487 2

For information on all Butterworth-Heinemann publications visit our website at www/bh.com

Typeset by Apek Digital Imaging Ltd., Nailsea, Bristol
Printed and bound in Great Britain

Contents

Preface vii

Acknowledgements xvii

1 What is Regulation? 1

2 Regulation and compliance in different markets 21

3 Compliance and operations 35

4 Client protection in the retail markets 51

5 Money laundering 61

6 Fraud and insider dealing 81

7 Operations and breaches of regulation 89

8 The future of regulation 105

Appendix A 113

Appendix B 115

Appendix C 145

Appendix D 173

Useful websites 177

Index 179

Please note:

If you have any difficulty in obtaining the reports/brochures mentioned in this book via their websites please contact the author of this book, David Loader, at DSC Portfolio Limited in London. Please use this Fax number: + 44 (0) 207 403 7004. The author will be happy to assist you in obtaining them.

Preface

Be honest, if you have just picked up this book and are reading this preface you are either supremely interested in regulation and compliance or you have probably picked up the wrong book!!

It's not that regulation and compliance is not an important subject or indeed that it is a boring, heavy subject (although there are those that think of it that way). It's more that it is just not everyone's favourite subject and so unless it is desperately essential, few will bother to delve too deeply into it. If you fall into this category, I very much hope you will stick with the book because it is time that the whole subject was looked at not from the compliance officers viewpoint or the regulators, but instead from the viewpoint of those that work in the operational areas of the business.

While we are going to look at rules, regulations, procedures and even the odd bit of law we are going to try and do it in a different way. Also there is very good reason why you should carry on reading this book. Operations, like any other part of an organization in the financial services industry has rules and regulations to comply with so best we find out what it is all about.

Although many view regulation as being about rooting out rogue traders and controlling speculators, its role is actually much more profound than this and without it many more so called scandals would undoubtedly occur. In essence the role of the regulator is akin to that of other Law enforcers; not much appreciated until something happens. Then without someone being prepared to uphold the Law there would be anarchy. In financial markets the regulators are viewed by some as being anything from a constraint on business to an ineffective massive cost burden for participants in the markets. The more enlightened have a different view.

In the first instance they must logically have a role in constraining business, particularly the kind of business that is excessive or hugely risky and badly controlled. The real regulatory question, given that a regulatory environment exists to ensure a market operates in a fair and orderly manner, is whether the regulators are able to constrain the kind of activity that causes unfair losses to vulnerable participants in the markets.

The fact that significant events like the collapse of Barings, Long Term Capital Management, Allied Irish, Enron, etc. have occurred and continue to occur leaves the regulator in a bit of a quandary. On the face of it they appear to be not regulating strongly enough and yet in many quarters there is considerable disquiet about the amount of regulatory influence there already is. Neither is it those on the 'shady' side of the market where regulation might be expected to receive little welcome who are concerned. Many major global banking organizations frequently complain about the time and money they have to invest just dealing with regulation. It should be pointed out that these banks would have a much more plausible case were it not for the numerous internal failures to control the greed and indifference to the rights and well being of customers, shareholders, etc.

One can discover just how poor the controls put in place by businesses can be by reading '*FIASCO. Guns, Booze and Bloodlust: the Truth about High Finance*' by Frank Partnoy (Profile Books, September 1998) that tells in graphic detail how dealers in a major U.S. bank would 'rip the faces off' their clients. This is by no means an isolated occurrence and few if any major firms are without their problems in managing a high risk, high reward business or indeed a client facing business where the primary responsibility is to the client.

Banks, brokers and fund managers have all suffered at the hands of unscrupulous traders, greedy dealers and corrupt operations staff.

We need to put this into perspective. It is a minority, albeit a seemingly increasing one, that is involved in fraud and deceit but that is not relevant. If one client is defrauded then the firm concerned is in question; if many clients are defrauded the firm loses credibility and probably its existence; if there is a systemic market-wide defrauding of clients the whole financial system becomes vulnerable.

And yet the financial markets are robust. Major problems, scandals, disasters like Maxwell, BCCI, Guiness, Barings have come and gone but the markets continue. It therefore seems that there is an acceptance that regulation and regulators can do only so much and as long as it seems that the rogues and the embezzlers and the sheer incompetent are in the main found out and dealt with, the occasional problem can be lived with. This is an interesting concept. Try telling a Mirror Group pensioner or a Barings bond holder that the occasional problem is OK!

Equally one only has to look at the revelations about research teams at the largest, and therefore supposedly better controlled and less risky, banks where some clients have been told one thing while the company told 'favoured clients' to take the opposite position in the market. It is issues like these that show why the regulator and regulation is desperately needed and why the regulator states that 'there is no such thing as an inadvertent breach of regulations'.

On the other hand there is a valid argument that regulation must be both effective and of benefit to the markets and the participants, including the banks, brokers and clients. It must also be neither master nor subservient and cannot be such a financial drain that it curtails legitimate and vital businesses.

In the U.K. regulation is now under a single body, The Financial Services Authority (FSA). Again it would seem on the face of it a highly logical situation, and yet some detractors quickly point out how much this has all cost to set up and how much it will cost in the future, and above all they point to the extensive power that the FSA has, power some feel is too great. Their arguments are often supported by highlighting the failures of regulators, and the FSA itself has had questions asked about its effectiveness in the case of the 'split caps', investment trusts that cross invested in each other and therefore collectively were highly vulnerable should one trust run into problems; where investors lost large sums of money in products that had been looked at by the FSA which concluded that there was no problem.

The perceived ineffectiveness, despite the huge costs to firms, to prevent situations happening is both a worry and can undermine the whole regulatory system. The problem it would seem is that the current level of regulation is not sufficient and yet more regulation would be fiercely opposed.

As we have just noted, the reaction of regulators to a problem has not always been good, the perception being that too little is done too late. When a scandal or disaster arises, the general view is that the industry was aware of what was happening but the regulator was powerless to act or, more likely, acted far too late. In the early days of regulation there were in most countries several regulatory agencies and this was the case in the U.K. until the collapse of Barings. Under new legislation introduced by the incoming Labour Government in 1997, the all encompassing Financial Services Authority, the FSA, was created to replace the previously separate regulatory bodies set up under previous financial market Acts.

It was suggested by some that the separation of regulatory responsibilities and powers had contributed to Barings demise. The rationale was that the apparent ineffectiveness of the Bank of England and the Securities and Futures Authority that regulated Barings banking and securities business to see what was happening and the failure to act appropriately would not have occurred if a single regulator had been in operation. With hindsight that may well have been the case and yet there have still been problems since Barings like the previously mentioned losses incurred by investors in 'split caps' where questions have been raised about the action or lack of it by the regulator. This suggests that a single regulator being in place is not necessarily any guarantee that no problems will arise. Equally there is some concern that major events have occurred on a global front in spite of more open exchange of information between regulators.

So is regulation effective?

The problem for the regulator is that unless total oversight of every transaction, account, business and individual can be made, there will always be rogue traders or more recent examples of failures of control like Enron and World.Com and even money laundering incidents. As such intense oversight is neither practical nor even desirable, the industry has to accept that the regulator can only do so much and the rest, in fact I would suggest, most of the responsibility lies with the firms and organizations themselves.

To put it into perspective, a rogue trader is down to a firm and whilst the regulator can put down requirements and guidelines on the firm that should prevent such a situation, it is the firm that fails in its responsibility. The role of the regulator in this case is to try to weed out firms that cannot, will not or do not do enough to prevent the rogue trader. Given that in many cases firms are apparently unaware of the rogue trader until the damage has been done, the regulator needs to be rigorous in monitoring the firm and vetting its procedures and controls. For operations teams this is significant. Their role in protecting the firm stems from the ability to manage critical processes like reconciliation, position agreements and the bank/*nostro* accounts efficiently and effectively. By seeing the actual result of transactions via the settlement process including payments and reconciled market positions, operations can be said to have the ultimate control function. Look at it this way, in the Barings scenario the daily payment of the margin calls on the derivatives positions gave a clear pointer to the situation the firm was getting into. The continuous outflow of funds could only have been to cover losses or for collateral against massive futures and options positions at the clearing house. Proper verification of the reason for the cash payments would have flagged the danger and impending disaster that was going to strike the bank. In no way and nowhere in the internal records and accounts at Barings could the apparent profits marry up to the cash outflow. Senior management clearly were at fault here because the business was not being managed and profits that could not have been right were accepted without adequate investigation into their merit.

Somewhere in the operations function the problem was almost certainly recognised and in all probability concerns raised. What happened to these highlighted concerns at higher levels, and the assumption here is that nothing much happened, caused the position to escalate out of control until eventually the bank collapsed. The Barings collapse was obviously a much more complex situation and indeed called into question the role of many organizations including the Bank of England and the auditors, internal compliance and risk management.

It is important to recognize that without effective input to the regulatory oversight process by the internal and external compliance and audit teams, plus the skill and experience of the operations managers and teams, there would be even greater and widespread abuse of the markets, client's assets and criminal activity in the financial markets. It is not surprising then that the issues surrounding the collapse of companies like Enron, etc., focus on the failure of the regulatory oversight by areas like audit, compliance and internal operations/accounts teams to identify and force correction of incorrect and deliberately misleading accounts, thereby allowing the company to appear solvent and profitable to the outside world.

However we need to clarify this point. Enrons *et al.*'s positions, assets, etc. may well have been agreed and reconciled by operations teams, but the resulting profits and losses may have been misrepresented in the accounts. Again there is going to be a highly complex series of situations that create something like an Enron including the structure of the business, management structure, reporting lines, etc. The production of, and indeed contribution to, invalid data would not, in all probability, have been apparent to those involved in the process. However once it had been formulated and reported to the regulatory authorities and the market by way of the published accounts the healthy, but false picture, was in the public domain. The investor, lending banks and indeed the regulators were thereby relying on the audit process to confirm that data recorded and reported as the true accounting records was indeed just that, and that the managers of the business had confirmed that they had discharged their duties competently.

The accounts were fabricated and the managers, at least some of them, were basically irresponsible, unfit to be managers, guilty of negligence and in all probability will be proven to have been party to criminal acts.

So much for corporate governance being entrusted to the so-called 'leaders of business', the same people who often publicly denounce the corruption that exists in emerging markets in other countries.

Again we need to put things in perspective. Not all businesses or managers are corrupt and as usual the innocent are damaged by the actions of the minority. However if that minority grows larger then the problem will in turn grow to catastrophic proportions. We will wait to see if the actions taken by the U.S. authorities and indeed President Bush can restore the image of the 'business leaders' and indeed the whole corporate market place.

Again looking at things in perspective, audit cannot be expected to uncover every problem, particularly if someone or group of people have the will and the means to hide or corrupt the data, and especially if someone in this group works in the audit team.

So therefore those with the ownership of the responsibility for the true and correct management of the business, including ensuring compliance with the regulatory authorities, are the directors and or owners, if it is not a publicly quoted company, of the business.

When they collectively or individually fail in their duty then there is a very major chance that disaster will happen. Worse still, that failure could be deliberate, in other words they are party to the deceit, criminal activity or manipulation of assets and records; for instance the recent disclosures about companies in the U.S. mentioned above or further back the Robert Maxwell scenario with the misuse (theft) of the assets of Mirror Group Pension Fund and the pensions mis-selling scandal in the U.K.

When these types of scenarios occur, the trust that shareholders and employees had in the Board of their company was shown to have been misplaced, but more crucially the whole credibility of the financial markets and the organizations operating in them is called into question.

So a problematic circle is created. Regulators need the help and support of the businesses to have a 'business friendly regulatory environment'. Some abuse the trust placed in them and the regulatory environment. Then a scandal or worse occurs and the majority are penalized as regulators react to criticism and apply more onerous regulations.

It is often the operations teams that bear most or at least some of the repercussions of greater regulatory oversight of the business. Therefore the understanding of regulatory issues and drivers is vitally important in operations teams and management.

Globally, regulation, whilst having the same core principles, works differently in different jurisdictions. Some have a more 'liberal' approach to the way in which markets operate and the clients are afforded greater protection in some markets than others. Again the operations manager needs to understand the important regulatory issues in the various markets in which the business operates.

In this book we look at regulation and compliance, but also try to look at things from another or a different angle, seeking to understand what regulation is about and how it affects operations functions rather than focusing solely on the detailed nitty gritty of the regulations themselves, although of course we have to understand what regulation is all about and how it works if we are to understand its impact on the operations function.

David Loader

Acknowledgements

I would like to thank Jeremy at the dsc.portfolio for some of the research and various organizations for their assistance and for the excellent material on their website including the Financial Services Authority, The Commodity Futures Trading Commission, The London Stock Exchange and AIMA. I would also like to thank Jennifer and Jackie at Elsevier for their patience!

Chapter 1

What is regulation?

Introduction

Regulation in the financial markets is focused on the activities of exchanges, clearing houses, banks, brokers and fund management, including areas like custody. This focus extends to the retail and wholesale market places as well as recognising the increasing globalisation of the financial markets, both investment and capital.

For operations teams one of the key interactions with the regulatory environment is in the protection of client assets. It is critically important for the credibility of the whole financial system, that the assets, securities and cash, as well as data about a client, are treated correctly and above all protected. Without this there would be little credibility attached to markets and without the direct and indirect participation of the client, the latter through personal investment as well as via retail funds and insurance companies, there would probably be no market.

Is this protection justified?

Yes, because there are undoubtedly many people and firms quite happy to relieve the odd pensioner, widow and orphan of whatever they possess. We might like to think that quaint morals like 'my word is my bond' still have a place in today's markets – dream on. That kind of scenario died along with trading floors, share certificates and long liquid lunches with your broker. Today we have mega-size businesses that have massive financial targets they fully expect to achieve. Dealers, sales teams, analysts, almost everyone from Board level director down is under huge pressure to deliver if they want their bonuses and, nowadays maybe even to keep their job.

Little wonder then that the 'client' is seen as a means of achieving the target rather than a valued customer whose interests should be uppermost.

A fund manager, one might imagine, will care about the clients' welfare, as after all it is the clients' money and assets they are managing. But then the manager has to deal with the bank or broker to get advice and to buy and sell the investments. The bank or broker may not have the same outlook!

Also the image of the trusted conservative investment manager is somewhat blown away by the pensions scandals and the other events that have seen the trusting investor lose their hard-earned savings through hopeless management and at times criminal activity.

Fund managers have seen the way in which traders have assumed star status and salaries to match. Not surprisingly they have thought why not me too? When such a venerable name in U.K. fund management as Mercury Asset Management is dragged into the Courts by a pension fund client and the media are more concerned about the personalities, life style and attire of two powerful ladies running the respective businesses we can conclude that the markets are not what they used to be.

Conduct and behaviour

We have seen that not all the scandals and deceit are down to traders. Salespeople and fund managers can stray from the path and so too can operations' managers. Every time there is a scandal, however great or small, the reputation of the financial markets is damaged. Sure, some of the largest banks that suffer 'problems' have the financial muscle to compensate anyone who has suffered a loss and equally can pay any fine the regulatory authorities may deem appropriate. However credibility also extends to the day-to-day and general activity in the markets and retail businesses where the orderly and correct process and behaviour is expected. The 'hard selling' associated with say, timeshare sales, is not acceptable in investment products, and so the regulations allow that the client must always have a period to change their mind and be able to do so without any financial loss.

Also the conduct of sales and trading is a key issue and unfair advantage created by exchange of confidential information between the sales and trading areas would be a breach of the rules. The concept of 'Chinese Walls' is about reducing conflicts of interest but there is also a need to prevent the exploitation of the client through mis-selling of products. In the U.K. there was a problem with this in terms of pensions and endowment policies as the following statement shows:

Pensions scandal costs £11.8bn
People were wrongly advised to move out of their occupational scheme

The Financial Services Authority (FSA) has announced that the pensions mis-selling scandal will have cost insurers and financial advisers at least £11.8bn in compensation payments.

More than one million customers who were mis-sold personal pensions and pension top-ups are in the process of receiving pay-outs.

> "This was a massive debacle. We just hope it never happens again"
>
> Malcolm McLean of the Pensions Advisory Service

The City watchdog said 1.7m consumers will have had their cases reviewed by the end of June and received their payments.

Since the beginning of the review into pensions mis-selling, the U.K.'s financial services watchdog has taken disciplinary action against 346 firms, resulting in fines totalling just under £10m.

In addition to a review of pensions, the FSA has also been undertaking a review of how top-up schemes – so-called free standing additional voluntary contributions or FSAVCs, were sold.

The Financial Services Authority has been looking at whether some people were wrongly advised to take out an FSAVC when they would have been better off joining their company's voluntary contribution scheme.

Extent of problem

Malcolm McLean of the Pensions Advisory Service (Opas) told BBC News Online that the overall costs announced on Thursday was indicative of the widespread mis-selling, which took place.

He said: 'It just shows the extent of the mis-selling. The whole point of this exercise was to put people back in the position they would have been in the first place.

'This was a massive debacle. It should never have happened and hopefully people will learn from it. We just hope it never happens again.'

Personal pension mis-selling?

The personal pensions mis-selling review began in 1994, and was aimed at people wrongly sold personal pensions between 29 April 1988 and 30 June 1994.

Mis-selling occurred when people who would have been financially better off at retirement in their employer's pension scheme were advised to leave or not join their employer's pension scheme.

The FSA prioritised older consumers or those near retirement.

The second part extended the review to younger consumers, typically in their 30s and 40s.

Topping up

The FSAVC review has looked at about 10% of FSAVC sales.

FSAVCs are a pension top-up policy which is taken out with an investment firm, and separate to an employer's pension scheme.

They are different to additional voluntary contributions (AVCs). This type of top-up policy is run by employers, and contributions are normally taken from pay.

The review has looked at situations where investors would have been better taking out these additional top-up schemes with their employer rather than a FSAVC.

Further information

Companies are in the process of writing to people and offering compensation

Firms involved in the mis-selling of FSAVCs and personal pensions mis-selling must complete their reviews and make their compensation offers by the end of 2002.

The FSA advises anyone who feels they were the victim of mis-selling to seek advice from its website.

So how does something like the pensions scandal illustrated above happen?

There are many possible reasons and these are not always down to deceit or anything illegal but more down to incompetence, pressures, errors and misunderstandings.

Of course it is not sufficient to say to an individual that 'we are sorry your pension is not worth anything, it was an error' and so the regulators view incompetence in general terms in the same way that they would view deliberate investing in an unsuitable product. More problematic is the issue of misunderstanding as here we are talking about whether a person understood what was being said to them by the salesperson and indeed did the salesperson understand what they were saying!!

For example recent results from government-initiated surveys suggest that few people really understand what a pension scheme actually is. It is understood that it provides a source of income in retirement but how it does so or how much must be saved to provide the required amount is not widely appreciated.

The reason that the pension mis-selling occurred is most likely a combination of situations rather than a single problem, particularly as it involved several different firms and a client base that lacked product knowledge. When there is a lack of real understanding, or a multiple failure of controls and business oversight, or an industry area acts in unison believing it is doing so correctly when in fact it is not, or a combination of these scenarios occurs, the outcome is likely to be that the investor loses.

It is to address this that the regulator creates requirements on the parties involved and then monitors their compliance with those requirements.

The requirements will cover ethics, business operation, marketing and sales, operational functions and client protection. Operations has a significant role to play in this but how does regulation impact?

To answer that question we need, as operations personnel, to understand the fundamentals of regulation and the regulatory environment.

Regulatory environment

The regulatory environment is complex as well as undergoing change. Significant change has already occurred in the United Kingdom where from the end of November 2001, a very new regulatory environment came into existence. The Financial Services Authority (FSA) has replaced the previous different regulatory bodies that covered particular parts of the financial markets industry (see Table 1.1).

This sole regulator role was formulated under The Financial Services and Markets Act 2000 (FSMA), and the risk-based approach to regulation adopted by the FSA is quite likely to become a role model for other financial markets across the world.

The FSA objectives are stated as:

1 **The Market Confidence Objective**
This objective seeks to maintain confidence in the financial system, which can be described as including exchanges and financial markets, regulated activities and other activities connected with financial markets and exchanges

2 **The Public Awareness Objective**
This objective seeks to promote the public understanding of the financial markets and includes promoting awareness of the benefits and risks associated with different kinds of investment or other financial dealing as well as provision of appropriate information and advice

3 **The Protection of Consumers Objective**
This objective seeks to provide appropriate degrees of protection for consumers and focuses on four specific factors; degrees of risk in different kinds of investment, differing degrees of experience and expertise that consumers have, the needs that consumers have for advice and accurate information, the general principle that consumers should take responsibility for their decisions

4 **The Reduction of Financial Crime Objective**
This objective seeks to reduce the extent to which it is possible for certain businesses to be used for a purpose connected with financial crime, which includes fraud or dishonesty; misconduct in a financial market; misuse of information relating to a financial market; handling the proceeds of crime

We will examine some of the issues arising from these objectives later in the book but clearly the FSA has powers far greater than the previous multiple regulators, and yet at the same time the FSA must work within strict guidelines laid down under FSMA 2000 as far as its role and functions are concerned.

Roles and functions of FSA

The FSA assumed the roles and functions of ten separate regulatory bodies involved in the financial markets. These were:

Table 1.1 The Financial Services Authority

Regulator	Regulated organisations
Building Societies Commission (BSC)	Building societies
Friendly Societies Commission (FSC)	Friendly societies
Insurance Directorate (ID) of the Department of Trade and Industry	Insurance companies
Investment Management Regulatory Organisation (IMRO)	Investment management
Personal Investment Authority (PIA)	Regulatory investment business
Registry of Friendly Societies (RFS)	Credit unions' supervision (and the registration and public records of building societies, friendly societies, industrial and provident societies and other mutual societies)
Securities and Futures Authority (SFA)	Investment business (including responsibility for supervising exchanges and clearing houses)
Supervision and Surveillance Division (S&S) of the Bank of England	Banking supervision (including the wholesale money market regimes)

The FSA will enforce its regulation under the powers granted to it under the Act. In turn, companies and organizations it regulates will be required to not only comply with these regulations but also the rules and regulations of other jurisdictions where they operate.

Regulation does of course differ for the various markets and services within the industry as the table of regulatory bodies prior to FSA showed. For instance Lloyds of London, operating in the insurance business would have some elements of regulation that were specific to that market and would not be relevant or appropriate for say retail investment business.

The role of the regulator is important in giving confidence to the market participants and also to the so-called end-users like institutional clients or customers. As such it will seek to provide rules that protect and at the same time reflect the nature of the business undertaken and risk appetite or otherwise of the investor or market participant. Obviously speculators take risks to try to make profits and the regulator does not seek to protect them from that objective. What it does do is to make sure that in taking that risk the speculator is not being taken advantage of. Equally a retired pensioner seeking to invest some money for the grandchildren does not expect to find that the hard-earned money has disappeared in ill-advised or unsuitably speculative dealings.

However the question of what is and is not a suitable product is quite difficult to determine. For instance, is a highly leveraged hedge fund suitable as an investment in a life fund portfolio? Well it may be if the amount of the portfolio represented by such an investment is very small because it gives the possibility of excellent, i.e. above average returns, at the risk of losing all or most of the assets invested. The balance of risk to reward in an investment is important and clearly defining that risk balance to a potential customer is equally important. Mandates, trust deeds, Scheme Particulars, Key Features Brochures, etc. give some indication of the nature of the product and guidance on what the types of investment are that is permitted, including the percentage of the fund property that can be put into a particular product or product type.

It may also stipulate what exchanges or markets can be used and how products can be used, for example derivatives may be authorised for use to hedge but not to take additional exposure.

However this guidance may be and often is fairly 'broad brush' and will not always convey the 'real' profile that the fund manager can or will take. Again we need to be careful here because the customer may not be familiar with the markets or products; this is highly likely in the case of something like derivatives, and so the regulator wants there to be more attention paid to warnings and also to assessing the suitability of the products for the customer. Hence we have the FSA requiring a *Warrants and Derivatives Warning Notice* (see Appendices A–C) to be sent to a client and received back signed by the client, as well as a suitable procedure internally to approve a client for the use of derivatives products.

There are so many types of products available that the assessment of what is and what is not suitable is not easy.

Independent Financial Advisors therefore have a difficult job but what about the advertisements in newspapers and periodicals or even junk mail that one sees for products? How can a potential customer determine if it is the right product or how can the supplier know if the potential customer is suitable for the product?

For instance hedge funds and other such types of products are ideal for certain types of investor in much the same way as a safe, secure and unspectacular government bond might be ideal for another type of investor.

The regulators approve products for general sale to the public and state how and under what terms and conditions the products can be sold. A hedge fund that is approved by the local regulator can be marketed to the public; however, if it is not authorised, it can only be sold direct to clients assumed to be technically aware or market specialists if indeed it can be sold at all.

Authorisation to market the product is one thing, but the marketing must be done in such a way that all material matters are made available to all the potential clients. The prospectus or offer for sale therefore becomes a crucially important document.

All regulation is trying to do is to make sure that the 'cap fits' and that no one is being in anyway put into a situation they do not understand or wanted to be in. Similarly, the many funds today are based on principles, such investments will only be in environmentally friendly companies, will recognise Islamic beliefs, are ethical funds and the like. Clearly an investor buying such an investment product is entitled to receive such a product, in the same way that the rights of the buyer of a new product like a car are protected by the right to compensation if the car is not as advertised and as expected.

Within regulatory frameworks, organizations such as exchanges and clearing houses establish rules and regulations that pertain to their members. It is important to recognize this in effect 'dual' regulatory situation whereby the FSA regulates the exchanges and the exchange members as businesses, and the exchange that in turn regulates their members' activity on the exchange (Figure 1.1).

From the operation managers' perspective this means that there are two different sets of regulations to consider. Firstly the FSA's direct regulation and then the indirect regulation via the exchanges/clearing

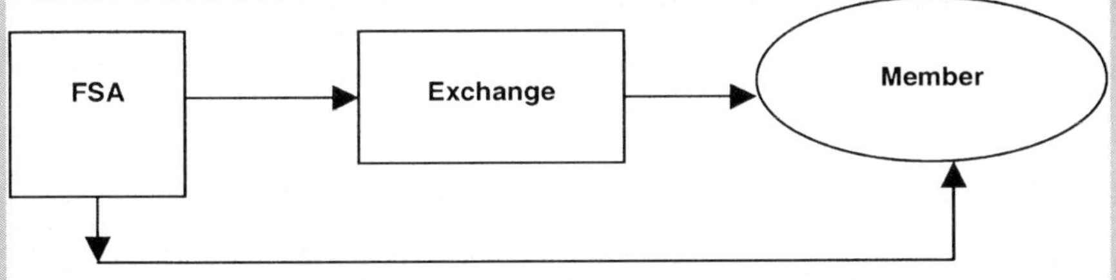

Figure 1.1

houses. Compliance with both is essential, particularly as under the risk-based approach taken by FSA, any transgression of the regulations will be severely punished.

Principles and conduct of business rules

The FSA has *Principles* and *Conduct of Business Rules* and it is here that the operations managers needs to focus their thoughts in terms of the requirements and procedures needed to meet their responsibilities.

The Principles set out the way in which the FSA believes firms and organizations should act in respect of regulations, clients, markets, etc., whilst the Conduct of Business Rules are designed to cover specific areas of activity that are undertaken.

Principles

The Principles, which are particularly relevant to operations teams, are:

Principle 6: Customers' Interests
Requires a firm to pay due regard to the interests of its customers and treat them fairly

Principle 7: Communication With Clients
A firm must pay due regard to the information needs of its clients and communicate information to them in a way which is clear, fair and not misleading

Principle 8: Conflicts of Interest
A firm must manage conflicts of interest fairly, both between itself and a customer and between one customer and another client.

Principle 9: Customers: Relationship of Trust
A firm must take reasonable care to ensure the suitability of its advice and discretionary decisions for any customer who is entitled to rely on its judgement

Principle 10: Clients' Assets

A firm must arrange adequate protection for clients' assets when it is responsible for them

Conduct of Business Rules

We need to look at some of the Conduct of Business Rules in more detail, as they are particularly relevant to operations teams.

The Conduct of Business Rules are:

The FSA Conduct of Business Rules cover the following (the rule number is shown on the left):

1 Application and general provisions
2 Clear, fair and not misleading communication
3 Financial promotion
4 Accepting customers
5 Advising and selling
6 Product disclosure and the customer's right to cancel or withdraw
7 Dealing and managing
8 Confirmation of transactions
9 Custody
10 Operators of collective investment schemes
11 Trustee and depositary activities
12 Lloyds

As one can imagine, each of these Rules has elements that will apply either directly or indirectly to operations teams but some have more relevance than others.

The FSA Conduct of Business Rules impact on the operations teams in a number of ways, for instance the custody rules apply to a firm when it is safeguarding and administering investments.

The description of custody and safekeeping, (COB 9) is given as:

> The regulated activity of safeguarding and administering investments covers both the safeguarding and administration of assets (without arranging) and arranging the safeguarding and administration of assets, when those assets are either safe custody investments or custody assets. A safe custody investment is a designated investment that a

firm receives or holds on behalf of a client. Custody assets include designated investments, and any other assets that the firm holds or may hold in the same portfolio as a designated investment held for or on behalf of the client.

The rules covering custody are related to the **FSA Principle 10**, which requires a firm to arrange adequate protection for assets for which it is responsible. As part of these protections, the custody rules require a firm to take appropriate steps to protect safe custody investments for which it is responsible.

The rules are designed primarily to restrict the commingling of client and firm's assets and minimise the risk of the client's safe custody investments being used by the firm without the client's agreement or contrary to the client's wishes, or being treated as the firm's assets in the event of its insolvency.

Given this point of view we can understand why operations teams must maintain segregation of assets and suitable records to show that this has been the case.

There are however, many caveats that apply to the COBs and so it is important that the reader studies the full Rules which are available at the FSA website. By way of example, we can look at the following under the heading **'Delivery versus payment transactions'**

9.1.13

A designated investment need not be treated as a safe custody investment in respect of a delivery versus payment transaction through a commercial settlement system if it is intended that the designated investment is either to be:

(1) in respect of a client's purchase, due to the client within one business day following the client's fulfilment of a payment obligation; or
(2) in respect of a client's sale, due to the firm within one business day following the fulfilment of a payment obligation; unless the delivery or payment by the firm does not occur by the close of business on the third business day following the date of payment or delivery of the designated investment by the client.

9.1.14

Until a transaction of the type described in COB 9.1.13R settles, a firm may segregate money (in accordance with the client money rules) instead of the client's safe custody investment.

Another example of how the Rules apply to the everyday operational processes is that given under 9.1.27:

> The rules governing the segregation, registration or recording, and holding of a client's safe custody investments require a clear distinction to be maintained, to the extent practicable, between safe custody investments held for the clients and those designated investments held for the firm.

The Rules also look specifically at assets being used for collateral purposes, something which most operations personnel are increasingly likely will come across.

9.4.5

The purpose of this section is to ensure that an appropriate level of protection is provided for those assets over which a client gives a firm certain rights. The arrangements covered by this section are those under which the firm is given a right to use the asset, and the firm treats the asset as if all legal title and associated rights to that asset had been transferred to the firm subject only to an obligation to return equivalent assets to the client upon satisfaction of the client's obligation to the firm. The rights covered in this section do not include those arrangements by which the firm has only a bare security interest in the client's asset (in which case the custody rules or client money rules apply).

9.4.6

Examples of the arrangements covered by this section include the taking of collateral by a firm, under the ISDA English Law (transfer of title) and the New York Law Credit Support Annexes (assuming the right to rehypothecate has not been disapplied).

9.4.7

This section recognises the need to apply a differing level of regulatory protection to the assets which form the basis of the two different types of arrangement described in COB 9.4.5G. Under the bare security interest arrangement, the asset continues to belong to the client until the firm's right to realise that asset crystallises (that is, on the client's default). But under a 'right to use arrangement', the client has transferred to the firm the legal title and associated rights to the asset, so that when the firm exercises its right to treat the asset as its own, the asset ceases to belong to the client and in effect becomes the firm's asset and is no longer in need of the full range of client asset protection.

The firm may exercise its right to treat the asset as its own by, for example, clearly so identifying the asset in its own books and records.

There are many more examples of areas of the Rules that would apply directly or indirectly to the operations team in their work but as I have said it is best that reader looks at the full COB's to ascertain which will be particularly relevant to their business.

The FSA, as previously noted may well become the template for other regulatory regimes around the world but for the present there is a variety of regulatory structures and issues for the manager to deal with.

Impact of regulation in the global markets

Regulation in global markets is on a country-by-country basis. The exception is in Europe where there is regulation covering the member states of the European Economic Community (EEC). Here there are various European Union Directives such as the **Investment Services Directive (ISD)** and the **Capital Adequacy Directive (CAD)**. The Investment Services Directive that must be complied with has as its objective the harmonisation of standards of regulation in investment businesses and therefore will allow firms established in any EU member state to conduct investment business in another EU state. The Capital Adequacy Directive establishes minimum funding requirements for all ISD businesses. There is also the **Second Banking Co-ordination Directive (2BCD)**, which permits a credit institution (bank) to be authorised in any one member state and offer services in another.

For the purposes of these directives the European Economic Area (EEA) is used and this comprises the 15 European Union Members, (Austria, Belgium, Denmark, Finland, France, Germany, Greece, Holland, Ireland, Italy, Luxemburg, Portugal, Spain, Sweden and the United Kingdom) plus Norway, Liechtenstein and Iceland.

In the United States of America there are two key regulatory bodies, *The Securities and Exchange Commission* (*SEC*) and the *Commodity Futures Trading Commission* (*CFTC*) and managers will need to be aware of their respective areas of control and the requirements on overseas firms and investors. In Japan there is the *Financial Services Agency* and as several leading international banks have found to their cost, breaching the rules is a costly, and in reputation terms, a disastrous experience. These and other major international regulatory structures are looked at in more detail in the next chapter.

Practical operations issues

One significant issue is that operations and compliance need to work together to ensure compliance with domestic and international regulation. As most organisations have a very broad brief in terms of their business, regulation can be varied dependent on the nature of the business, whether it deals for or with clients and whether it is transacting business internationally. Compliance is a vital function in helping organisations overcome a potentially difficult and dangerous business issue and yet the role of compliance is not always understood.

The role can be defined as:

> The task of ensuring that an organisation complies with the rules of any relevant regulatory authority where that organisation carries on business and the responsibility to ensure that the organisation adheres to the rules of any exchanges of which it is a member or where it transacts business.

In many cases it also monitors compliance with internal rules and controls over the business and works closely with audit, risk management and legal departments. It will most likely be involved in seeking to prevent and identify criminal acts such as money laundering.

In another book in this series *Relationship and Resource Management in Operations* the need for operations managers and teams to view compliance in a positive rather than negative way was highlighted. Understanding the role of compliance is important and likewise compliance needs to ensure that operations teams have the necessary information and guidance in respect of the regulatory implications that affect them such as reporting, client money rules, etc.

Compliance can be said to have some principal responsibilities that would include:

1 Creating and maintaining internal rules and procedures to ensure compliance with relevant regulatory requirements
2 Ensuring that business is conducted in accordance with the regulations
3 Liaising with trading, sales and operational areas to ensure new services and products will meet any regulatory requirements
4 Creating awareness and an understanding of the need for compliance with internal and external rules

The compliance officer has responsibility to ensure that both internal and external 'regulation' is complied with. The way in which this is done varies from business to business. In a small operation the compliance role may be relatively easy as there is immediate oversight of what is going on in the business. A larger operation may require a compliance team or department to oversee the various types of business and regulatory issues that arise. As the responsibility is not just about ensuring compliance with regulation but also about protecting the business, compliance is a complex function.

In essence it relies on quality information, high levels of understanding of the regulatory issues at all levels in the business and strong enforcement of the internal and external regulations, rules and policies.

The interaction between the compliance officer/team and the operations manager/team is crucially important to the business as a whole, and the importance of this relationship must be conveyed to all employees.

In Chapter 7 we look at what happens when there are inadvertent breaches of regulations, or for that matter internal controls, but in general terms the need is for operations teams to understand that the impact of poor compliance is going to be:

1. **Possible financial penalties (fines)**
2. **Reputation damage (public reprimand)**
3. **Loss of clients (concerns about risk)**
4. **Problems with credit (reluctance of counterparties to extend credit lines)**

Summary

In summary then regulation is about the determining of rules that are needed to govern the conduct of firms and individuals in their business, determining what level of protection individuals and organisations should expect, and providing and appointing representatives to ensure that the various rules and regulations are enforced, monitored and complied with.

Regulation seeks to stabalise market and investment environments and to prevent the types of criminal activities where the financial services industry might present opportunities like insider dealing, money laundering and mis-selling of products. It also seeks to generate confidence in the markets and market support processes so that all participants believe that they are operating in, as far as is possible to achieve, a fair and safe environment.

Chapter 2

Regulation and compliance in different markets

Introduction

There are different regulatory regimes in each market. There can be more than one regulator as in the United States or a single all-powerful regulator as in the United Kingdom. There is also the European Commission, which publishes Directives that affect the member States of the European Union.

So what is the implication for operations teams and managers?

We look at this in more detail later in the chapter but suffice it to say that there are real dangers for a business if for some reason a regulation applying to a particular product or service is breached and ignorance is no defence. Even if it were as far as the regulator was concerned, the impact on the firm's reputation will be highly damaging anyway.

To compound the challenge that the operations teams has of knowing the main regulatory issues of each jurisdiction in which they do business, they also have to cope with change.

Changes have been taking place in the regulatory environment for some years and in several countries. As well as the creation of the Financial Services Authority in the United Kingdom, in Germany for instance the *Bundesanstalt für Finanzdienstleistungsaufsicht (BAFin)*, the "BAFin – German Financial Supervisory Authority" has been created by the result of a merger (1 May 2002) between the Federal Banking Supervisory Office (*Bundesaufsichtsamt für das Kreditwesen* – BAKred), the Federal Insurance Supervisory Office (*Bundesaufsichtamt für das Versicherungswesen* – BAV) and the Federal Securities Supervisory Office (*Bundesaufsichtsamt für den Wertpapierhandel* – BAWe).

The European regulators are shown in Table 2.1. This gives the Supervisory Authorities of the EU Members plus those of the Associate Member countries

An overview of European regulation

The European Union was established to provide, amongst other things, free movement of goods and services throughout all member states. It achieves this through a harmonisation of common standards by each country.

These standards are contained in Directives which are incorporated into each country's own legislative system.

Investment Services Directive (ISD)

Such a Directive is the Investment Services Directive (ISD) which was incorporated into the U.K. regulatory system at the beginning of 1996.

The ISD contains standards required for business providing investment services. Regulation is split between:

Home State: the country of a firm's head office and registered office. It is responsible for authorisation and capital adequacy
Host State: any other member state in which the firm operates. It is responsible for the Conduct of Business Rules

Table 2.1 European regulators

Country	Regulator	Mnemonic
Austria	Austrian Securities Authority	ASA
Belgium	The Banking and Finance Commission	BFC
Cyprus	The Cyprus Securities Commission	
Denmark	The Danish Supervisory Authority	
Finland	The Financial Supervision Authority	FSA
France	The Commission des Operations de Bourse	COB
Germany	The Bundesaufsichtsamt fur den Westpapierhandel	BAWe
Greece	The Capital Market Commission	CMC
Hungary	The Hungarian Financial Supervisory Authority	
Iceland	Fjarmalaeftirlitio, The Financial Supervisory Authority	FME
Ireland	The Central Bank of Ireland	
Italy	The Commissions Nazionale per le Societa e la Borsa	CONSOB
Luxembourg	The Commission de Surveillance du Secteur Financier	
Netherlands	Securities Board of the Netherlands	STE
Norway	Kredittilsynet	
Poland	The Polish Securities and Exchange Commission	
Portugal	The Portuguese Securities Market Commission	CMVM

Table 2.1 Continued

Country	Regulator	Mnemonic
Slovenia	The Slovenia Securities Market Agency	
Spain	The Commission Nacional del Mercado de Valores	CNMV
Sweden	Finansinspektionen, the Swedish Financial Supervisory Authority	
Switzerland	The Swiss Federal Banking Commission	SFBC
United Kingdom	Financial Services Authority	FSA

Source: The Federation of European Stock Exchanges (as at August 2002)

This enables any business authorised in one member state to conduct business in another member state without seeking further authorisation. It is known as the "single passport."

The Capital Adequacy Directive (CAD)

The Capital Adequacy Directive (CAD) is, like the ISD, a major component of the Single European Market in financial services.

CAD sets common minimum capital standards for firms, establishing a broadly level playing field between non-bank investment firms and banks which trade in the financial markets.

An overview of regulation in the United States

In the United Sates the regulatory framework is different. Here two key regulators, The Securities and Exchange Commission (SEC) and the Commodity Futures Trading Commission plus various other

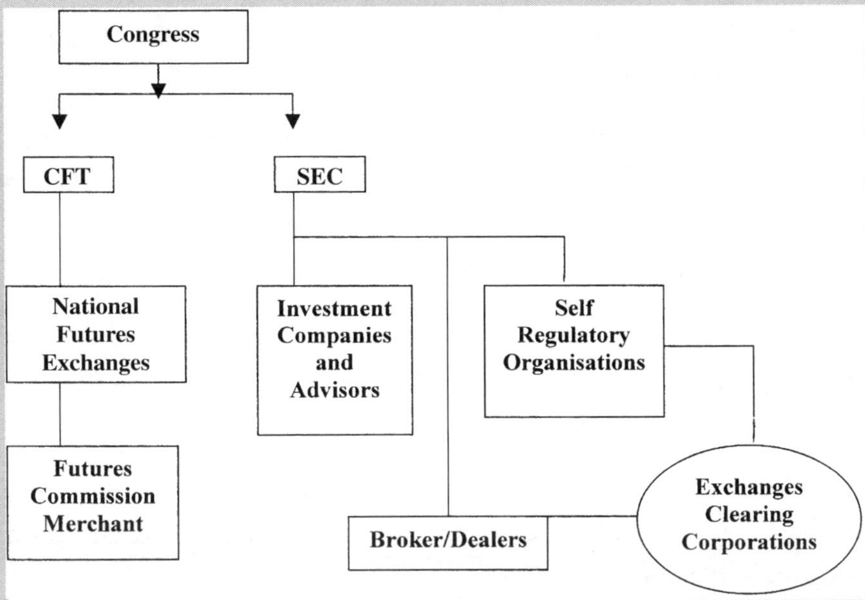

Figure 2.1 Structure of regulation in the United States

Source: ISSA Handbook/the dsc.portfolio

national and State regulatory bodies oversee the financial markets (see Figure 2.1).

Securities and Exchange Commission (SEC)

The scope of the SEC includes:

- Provides for oversight of brokers, dealers, clearing houses, associations and exchanges regulated under the Securities Exchange Act of 1934
- Enforces customer protection rules
- Provides for registration and regulation of investment companies such as mutual funds, including acceptable locations to hold fund assets
- Provides for registration and regulation of investment advisors
- Power of enforcement and regulation

- Suspends or revokes registrations of brokers, dealers, investment companies and investment advisors who wilfully engage in prohibited acts and practices

The SEC is empowered under the Securities Act of 1933 and the Securities Exchange Act of 1934 as well as the Investment Company Act of 1940 and the Investment Advisors Act 1940.

Commodity Futures Trading Commission (CFTC)

Operating under the Commodity Futures Trading Commission Act of 1974 and the CFMA200, the CFTC:

- Regulates trading of various U.S. futures exchanges, public brokerage houses, futures commission merchants and commodity trading advisors
- Has power of enforcement and regulation for approving rules under which a futures exchange proposes to operate
- Monitors the various futures exchanges enforcement of rules such as client money segregation
- Investigates potential violations
- Reviews terms or proposed new futures contracts
- Suspends or revokes registrations

Under Congress are also such bodies as the Office of Thrift Supervision, the Federal Reserve System, Federal Deposit Insurance Corp and the Office of the Comptroller of the Currency.

The CFMA 2000 set out a new framework

In the same way that other aspects of the financial markets change, so too does regulation, as can be illustrated by the Commodity Futures Modernization Act (CFMA 2000) that was passed in the United States in 2000 and relates to derivatives.

Like the Financial Services Markets Act and Conduct of Business Rules in the U.K., the CFMA 2000 has clear objectives to make the markets better controlled and therefore safer for participants. It is also, like its U.K. counterparts, a very long document.

Appendix D is an extract taken from the Bill which shows the objectives, etc., and which once again the reader is advised to at least look at in the context of areas that would apply to their business. There are details of the Commodity Futures Trading Commission (CFTC) and the full Act document can be accessed via their website, which is worth a visit.

In the U.S., derivatives are regulated by both the SEC (equity related) and CFTC (bonds, commodities and financials).

Under Section 132 of the Federal Deposit Insurance Corporation Improvement Act of 1991 there was a requirement on each appropriate federal banking agency to establish standards in three areas for the institutions under its jurisdiction. No statutory authority to exempt is permitted, therefore all federally insured depository institutions, including all Federal Reserve Member banks and all national banks must adhere to these standards.

These federal banking agencies, the Federal Reserve Board, the Office ofThrift Supervision and the Federal Deposit Insurance Corp, issues guidelines rather that regulation to establish the standards.

Broadly speaking this requires banking institutions to have in place controls and information systems that are:

- Appropriate to the size of activities
- Appropriate to the nature, scope and risk of the activities
- Controls and systems that provide for an organisational structure with clear lines of authority and responsibility for monitoring and adherence to established policies
- Effective risk assessment
- Timely and accurate financial, operational and regulatory reports
- Adequate procedures to safeguard and manage assets
- Compliance with applicable laws and regulation

In 1998, the United States federal banking supervisors, approved the *Supervisory Policy Statement on Investment Securities and End-User Derivatives Activities*, which provides guidance on sound practices for managing the risks of investment securities.

Amongst the guidelines contained in the policy statement are:

- Institutions should have programmes to manage the market, credit, liquidity, legal, operational and other risks of investment securities and end-user derivatives
- Policies should identify relevant investment objectives, constraints and guidelines for the acquisition and ongoing management of derivative instruments
- Policies should identify risks prior to the transaction and periodically after
- Adequate control oversight to ensure compliance with, and appropriateness of, investment policies, procedures and limits
- The appropriateness of the risk management systems to the activities
- Timeliness, integrity and usefulness of reports to senior management

We can see how the U.S. regulatory structure is different from that of the FSA in the U.K. but what about regulation in Asia Pacific?

Overview of regulation in Asia Pacific

The Asia-Pacific financial markets are, like the countries themselves, very individual. To understand the regulatory implications of business in this vast and diverse area we can begin by looking at the environment in Japan and first of all consider the way in which the Japanese regulatory authority, *The Financial Services Agency (JFSA)*, approaches the selling of securities to Japanese clients by overseas companies, in other words cross-border trading.

Look at the following statement from the JFSA:

The Guideline on cross-border securities transaction via internet by foreign securities firms based on Article 3 of the law on foreign securities firms

1 Basic Idea

Based on Article 3 of the Law on Foreign Securities Firms, unless a foreign broker-dealer registers the main branch in Japan with JFSA, a foreign broker-dealer is not allowed to engage in securities transactions with residents in Japan.

On the other hand, based on Article 2 Paragraph 2 of the Cabinet Order for the Enforcement of the Law on Foreign Securities Firms, even non-registered foreign broker-dealers are allowed to engage in securities transaction if they receive orders from investors in Japan without the direct 'solicitation' to them. The issue, therefore, is whether JFSA would consider a broker-dealer's Web site to be the 'solicitation', the attempt to induce securities transactions with Japanese investors.

2 Cross-Border Securities Transaction via Internet by Foreign Securities Firms

As a rule, a broker-dealer's advertisement on Internet Web sites such as the offer of market information, real-time or delayed quote information, or instructions on how to order, falls under the 'solicitation', that is, an advertisement about securities transaction in newspaper, magazine, television, radio or other related media based on Article 7 Item 1 of the Ordinance of the Prime Minister's Office on Foreign Securities Firms.

In spite of the above, the JFSA will not consider foreign broker-dealer's advertisement on an Internet Web site to constitute a 'solicitation', that is an attempt to induce securities transactions with residents in Japan, only if the foreign broker-dealer takes the following appropriate and rational measures designed to exclude the possibility of securities transactions with residents in Japan:

(1) Disclaimer

The Web site must have a prominent disclaimer which makes it clear that the offer is not aimed at residents in Japan.

- The JFSA will take into account the following factors in order to determine whether the disclaimer is adequate or not.

  The disclaimer should be seen without any special operation other than viewing the Web site.

The disclaimer should be described in the same language as the rest of the Web site.

(2) Measures designed to avoid securities transaction with residents in Japan

The measures must be designed to avoid dealing with persons in Japan.

- The JFSA will take into account the following factors in order to determine whether the measures are adequate or not.

  The broker-dealer should implement appropriate procedures to determine a potential customer's residence, by requiring them to provide their mailing address, e-mail address, payment or other information.

    The broker-dealer should prepare the appropriate procedures for rejecting an order reasonably recognized as being sent from Japan.

    The broker-dealer should not implement such measures as establishing a call-center in Japan or hypertext linked to the portal sites targeting to Japanese residents.

The above procedures are not definitive. The JFSA, therefore, will accept equivalent or more effective measures than those stated above.

The JFSA will consider a Web site to be a solicitation if the broker-dealer should fail to implement the appropriate measures mentioned above. In this case, the broker-dealer is required to prove that any transactions with residents of Japan took place without solicitation.

Source: JFSA website

Regulation in Japan is an issue that several major global investment banks have run into problems with (see Appendices).

Licences have been suspended and damage done to the creditability of the firm concerned making it difficult to build the business in Japan. Yet the regulation in connection with cross-border transactions outlined above is fairly straightforward and logical and only requires an operations manager and compliance officer to have and monitor routine procedures.

Operational implications

The operational implications of cross-border trading can be considerable.

The operations manager and compliance officer must work closely to ensure that the possible rules and regulations that could occur in the structure shown above are fully understood and, of course, complied with.

Anyone that is familiar with the financial markets and keeps abreast through reading the *Financial Times, Wall Street Journal, Straits Times,* etc. of the events that are occurring in the Asia-Pacific region will know that various foreign and domestic banks have fallen foul of the local regulators. This is particularly true but is not restricted to Japan. The implications of scandals and other market abuses for investor confidence in the markets are fairly obvious. So too is the impact on an individual organisation. Suspension, revocation of licences, fines are likely outcomes. Internally 'heads will roll' and reputation is certainly damaged, sometimes irretrievably.

In December 2002, the full extent of the implications for a firm that is involved in a breach of regulations was perhaps graphically illustrated when the Financial Services Authority in the U.K. levied a record fine of £4m on Credit Suisse First Boston for its breaches of the regulatory environment in Japan.

As the *Financial Times* of 20 December 2002 reported under the headline '*FSA imposes record £4m fine of CSFB*', the firm had been given the penalty following an investigation that revealed the investment bank deliberately concealed documents and other evidence in order to mislead Japan's main regulator, the Financial Services Agency.

The Japan FSA had already fined CSFB Y40m in March 2001 for related events unearthed in 1999 and has subsequently revoked the licence of CSFB's derivatives arm, Credit Suisse Financial Products

The fine on CSFB was twice that previously levied by the FSA and sends a clear message. The previous record fines of £2m were levied on Morgan Grenfell for the scandal surrounding the activities of fund manager Peter Young and Royal Scottish Assurance for mispricing endowments.

An interesting point noted in the Lombard column of the F.T. was that the events happened in a period from 1995 to 1998 and CSFB is no longer under the same management.

Was the level of the fine, or even the fine itself justified under these circumstances?

Given that in this chapter, I have stressed the importance of credibility, reputation, etc. it would seem that an incidence of a firm apparently deliberately misleading a regulator must be considered a very serious issue for the markets as a whole. On that basis the fine would seem to be appropriate both as a punishment and as a deterrent.

Whilst we are on the subject, record fines are also likely to be levied in the United States on firms that have been involved in the various corporate scandals like Enron that have recently occurred. These are likely to be far greater than that imposed by the U.K. FSA on CSFB but then again the seriousness of the events is far greater too.

Summary

The global regulatory environment creates a major challenge for firms, compliance officers and operations teams.

It is not just about the differences or the complexities but more about the problems of non-compliance. Any firm undertaking client business in international markets has many issues to overcome and particularly needs to pay attention to matters affecting client protection.

As 'new' products and services evolve and the industry moves more and more into the outsourcing of operational functions, so the regulatory and compliance challenge grows. For example, prime brokerage services and fund administration are two areas that need to be fully conversant with the operational issues of regulation. So too of course do custodians.

Chapter 3

Compliance and operations

Operations teams as a key component of a business in the financial markets are responsible for processes and procedures that are subject to regulation, and as we have already noted they are also responsible for several potential risk management controls. Compliance with both of these is obviously essential and the operations managers role in this is a crucial one.

What exactly are operations teams complying with?

Essentially they are complying with elements of the Conduct of Business (COB) rules in the U.K. or their equivalent in other jurisdictions, other rules and regulations laid down by a national regulatory body in any markets where business is being carried out, any Law that pertains to the transaction of business including those relevant to money laundering, Company Law and Trusts, the rules and regulations of exchanges, clearing houses and other institutions that a firm might be a member of and the membership terms of any industry association. As such this offers a very broad and complex challenge.

The various rules and regulations affecting firms operating in the financial markets vary dependent on the type of business being undertaken. A large investment bank that has a principal trading capability, institutional and private client business and also a retail and fund management business, will have many different regulatory issues to contend with in general terms and also in operational terms.

Organisations like custodians have regulation to comply with as will specialist product firms like hedge funds. The degree of regulation varies and so too does the amount of regulation that operations teams are directly involved with.

So what in general terms does an operations team comply with?

Client money and assets

Well firstly, the protection of client assets because as we noted in chapter (1?) this is a core objective of regulation in the financial markets. Every day an operations team will be dealing with clients' assets unless it is a solely proprietary business. It is most likely that the assets will be 'managed' to ensure that there is maximum return available for the client and of course the assets may be held by the firm as collateral. In either case they belong to the client and as beneficial owner, all benefits accruing are due to the client. In certain circumstances a client may have agreed to waive their rights to protection, but not to the benefits that might accrue and therefore the operations team must ensure that the client receives all benefits. This is important as any failure by the firm to do so will be viewed as a risk to the client and most likely will be a breach of regulation.

Segregation of client assets from those of the firm is central to the protection, as obviously the client should not suffer a loss of their assets if the firm holding them ceases to trade either voluntarily or through bankruptcy or even through regulatory action like a withdrawal of a licence to operate.

In the U.K. under the FSA Conduct of Business (COB) rules client money is held on trust. The effect of this is broadly speaking;

(a) It must be held in a segregate client bank account, that is, an account appropriately designated as containing client money or in a money market deposit identified as client money
(b) The account must normally be with an 'approved bank', that is, in practice, broadly a bank or building society authorised under

the FSMA; a European Economic Area (EEA) bank; or a bank established elsewhere that meets the criteria of substance.(as defined under approved banks). If a non-U.K. account is used, the client must be notified and a risk warning given

(c) Client money may be held in a non-approved bank only in limited circumstances, where required for the settlement of transactions, or receipt of income, outside the U.K.: risk warnings must be given and the consent of private customers obtained

(d) The bank must acknowledge the basis on which the client money is held. If it fails to do so the account must be closed in the case of a U.K. account or the client notified in any other case

(e) In the case of a private customer, a firm must account to the customer for all interest earned on his money, unless it has notified him in writing of an alternative position

The implications for the operations team are that client money must be:

1 Recognised
2 Kept separate from the firms money
3 Routed to a segregated account at an approved organisation
4 If a non-approved bank is being used the relevant warning must be given and consent obtained from the client
5 Interest must be accounted for unless otherwise agreed with the client

As a result of this the firm will have established relationships with approved banks, etc. and organised designated client money accounts. These will be recorded in the procedure documentation manual and provided adequate controls and reconciliation takes place, there should be little difficulty complying with the rules.

However, there are other issues that need to be considered not least the rules pertaining to:

1 Payments into client accounts
2 Money ceasing to be client money

3 Client money calculations/reconciliations
4 Transfer of client assets to third parties
5 Cash payments
6 Use of collateral

Before we look at these in detail, what is client money?

Client money

The COB provisions are designed to apply where a firm receives or 'holds' money from or on behalf of a client, be it a private client or in principle a market counterparty in the course of or in connection with designated investment business. If the firm has a client with money held at third party, rather than the firm where the third party is holding money for a client where there is a direct accountability to the client, the firm does not have to treat the money as client money; however, if the account at the third party is for the firm then the rules will apply. This stops firms avoiding the client money rules by transferring money to another party.

Exceptions

Naturally enough as with most regulation and rules there are some exceptions and client money is, if you will pardon the term, no exception.

Exceptions to the rules include cheques that are made out to another party, for instance a product provider, and are passed through the firm. They also include permitted activities of a life office or friendly society where these companies deal with the client on a principal basis and do not hold money on their behalf on a long-term basis.

In addition money held by an approved bank in an account with itself is not usually client money and clients must be notified that it is not held on trust, and certain types of market counterparty or intermediate customers may opt out of the client money rules provided this is recorded in writing as acknowledging the money will not be segregated and will therefore only rank as a general creditor of the firm in the event of it ceasing business.

An example of the problems that can occur when a client opts out of the protection afforded by client money segregation, concerned the demise of a derivatives clearing firm that had several individuals as clients who lost money when the firm was hit by a massive default by one of its clients. The firm went out of business and as the individuals had opted out of the client money rules their money was not segregated.

There are other exceptions and relaxations to the client money rules and I would suggest that the reader obtains a copy of the excellent *A Practioners Guide to the FSA Rule Handbook*, published by City and Financial Publishing, which explains the regulations in more detail.

Coming back to the issues for the operations manager, it will be important that staff understand the client money rules sufficiently to be able to identify which clients have segregation and what happens to payments, etc., to which clients the rules do not apply and also implications of cross-border trades where money may be transferred to an agent. We also need to ensure an understanding of the client money calculations and the issues surrounding the use of collateral

Payments of money into client accounts should normally be paid into a client bank within one business day. In general terms the larger, more complex businesses will use an 'alternative' approach, which involves the paying in and out of money to clients via the firm's accounts with a daily transfer of funds to and from its client bank accounts, such that it complies with the client money, calculation. At some point money can cease to be client money the obvious time being when the money is paid to the client or their representative, for instance a custodian, but also when it is paid to the firm to settle for instance a fee or commission.

Money ceasing to be client money is important as it no longer figures in the client money calculation the firm must carry out. The client money calculation involves ensuring on a daily basis that the firm has sufficient funds available to meet all its obligations to its clients. Any shortfall must be made good by the firm so that where, for instance, a settlement of a trade has taken place in the market but the client has not made the money available, another client's money is not used to cover the settlement. The firm will have to put its own money into the client account and will presumably charge the client until the client's funds are received, otherwise it is effectively providing interest-free financing of the client's trades. Sometimes the firm will need to pay away client assets to another party as for instance as collateral against a margin call. This complicates matters as the receiving party, for instance a clearing house, may be dealing with the firm as a principal. An example of this is where the clearing house maintains separate accounts for the firm's principal and client positions but only recognises the firm, as its member, and holds them liable for all obligations due to the clearing house. The extent to which the client's money is segregated is important and where the party has the right to offset money held against other accounts, the situation is that either the firm must cease to use that party or, as would be the case if such a situation occurred with an exchange/clearing house, the firm must notify the client

Operationally, the calculation of client money and the reconciliation of the firm's own records with that of the underlying bank statements, as well as ensuring agents segregate money, or if that is not the case, then the clients are notified of any situation where segregation is not in place, are very important as any breach of the client money rules is a serious situation and will be treated as such by the regulator.

Collateral

The use of collateral to cover a client's obligations is a common enough occurrence but how is this viewed in terms of protection for the client? Assets and money are used either on the basis of being under a simple charge to the firm, enforceable in the case of a default by the client, or are used on the basis of being rehypothecated whereby the asset is treated as the firms' and used as collateral against the client's liabilities at, say, a clearing house.

In both cases the custody or client money rules would apply, and in the latter case the firm must ensure it maintains adequate records to ensure, amongst other things, that it can meet its obligation to return the asset to the client.

So, understanding the client money rules and developing procedures to ensure compliance with them is a fundamental task of the operations manager. As each financial market place may have differing rules and practices this becomes a significant challenge.

Regulators in many jurisdictions require firms to provide details of transactions they undertake and again the operations function is involved in ensuring the firm is complying.

Transaction reporting

Firms need to comply with the transaction reporting requirements of regulators in various market places. Transactions are monitored for a variety of reasons including risk, market manipulation and insider dealing. In order to ensure that a market place is operated in a fair and orderly manner, regulators monitor not only transactions but also rule breaches and position taking. The latter is primarily about possible insider dealing but is also about the exposure of a firm in comparison to its financial position, thus we have Capital Adequacy Directive (CAD).

Operations are involved in the process of transaction settlement and record keeping so naturally they have, or are certainly likely to have, some involvement in transaction reporting. In many markets transaction reporting is viewed as part of the trade cycle for that market. The supervision or surveillance of the business of its members by the exchange or other regulatory body is about reputation and integrity.

As such there will be a timeframe within and by which the member must report all its transactions.

The actual mechanism for trade reporting will vary from market to market. It may be automated so that an electronic market automatically forwards details of trades executed by members on the exchange dealing system. In this case there is no requirement for the member to report trades separately. Several markets operate such a system like *The Stock Exchange Electronic Trading System (SETS)* in the U.K.

Alternatively a message originated by the member may serve to provide the matching process and simultaneously will report the trade to the regulator. An example of this would be the International Securities Market Association (ISMA) *Trax* system. National central securities depositories may also forward details of settled trades to the regulator on receipt of valid settlement instructions from the member. Figure 3.1 illustrates these possible scenarios.

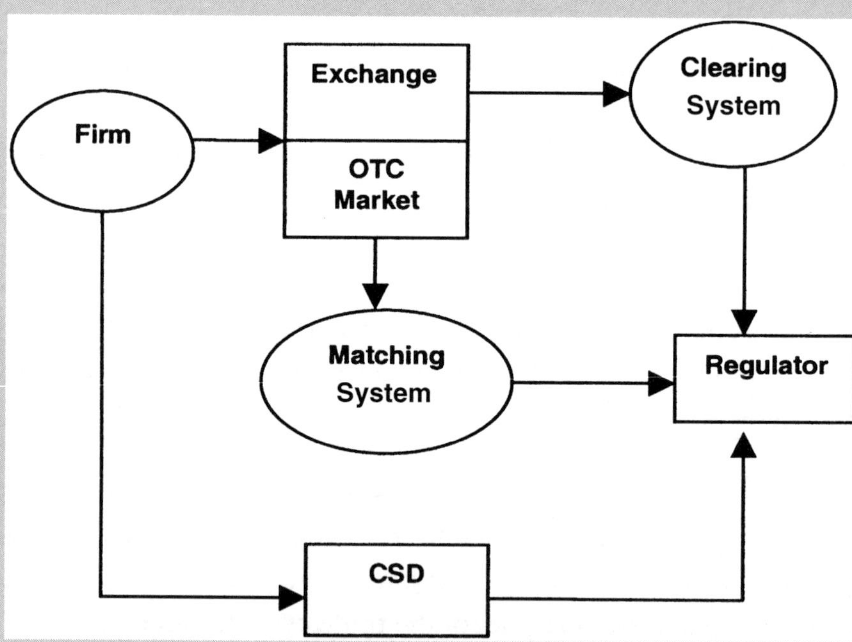

Figure 3.1

What data is needed in a trade report to a regulator?

In general terms the type of data that needs to be submitted will include:

- Whether the trade is principal or agency
- Date
- Time
- Value date of the trade
- Buy or sell
- Quantity
- Security
- Price
- Counterparty

This data as we have said is used by the regulator to highlight exceptions that might indicate manipulation, illegal activity, large exposure, etc. The major markets like the New York Stock Exchange, the Australian Stock Exchange, etc. have systems that automatically scan the vast amounts of data being submitted daily for abnormal trading patterns, etc. It is obvious that in the more volatile markets there will be significant changes in price, size of transaction, etc. and the regulators need to be able to identify 'normal' activity as distinct from potentially questionable trading.

Regulation in custody

Until fairly recently custody in the U.K. perspective was not a regulated business. Today the situation is very different in the U.K. and overseas.

As a significant part of the overall process in financial market activity, credibility in custody and safekeeping is of paramount importance. As custody is about investors assets and rights, the protection of those assets and rights is a key regulatory requirement.

Whilst there are the governing laws of the jurisdiction of the investor and the custodian to be complied with, there are also the agreements between the investor and the custodian that must also be complied with. This can be further complicated by the situation regarding a custodian that is providing a global custody facility as they will have agreements with sub-custodians.

In essence then, the custodian is faced with compliance issues covering the regulatory and reporting obligations of the countries in which they and the investor are based, the legal agreement with the investor/customer and any agreement with a sub-custodian.

The content of the agreement between the custodian and customer is often referred to as a prime agreement and may be drafted by either the custodian or customer. Most custodians have formal agreements that reflect the roles and responsibilities as they see them and which suits them, whilst the customer will naturally have their own version that has similar objectives. The result perhaps unsurprisingly is the final agreement is negotiated and is often an acceptable combination of the clauses and requirements of both parties.

Operationally the agreements, although they are negotiated customer by customer and therefore vary, will have certain fundamental provisions. These can be summarised as:

- Receipt of assets
- Authorised instructions
- Actions in response to instructions
- Actions to be taken without instruction
- Reporting requirements
- Use of securities depositories
- Liability of standard of care
- The choice of law and administrative provisions

These provisions are designed to cover the primary areas where the custodian is involved with the customer so that for instance, both parties are quite clear on what constitutes an authorised instruction, including method of delivery and which people are authorised to make an instruction. Provided that the custodian complies with this provision both the customer and the custodian are protected against possible fraud.

The Sub-Custody Agreement will also be negotiated and therefore will vary from market to market, but the provisions in the Prime Agreement will also apply in this agreement and so of course will any local regulation in the relevant jurisdiction.

The agreements and the internal procedures of the custodian are designed to meet not only regulatory requirements but also risk. Two key risks are those associated with the location of the investment, Country Risk and with the risks specific to the use of a sub-custodian, Sub-Custody Risk.

Many jurisdictions have regulatory requirements governing the evaluation of these risks and what firm is or is not acceptable as a counterparty. An example would be the United States where the SEC mandates such an evaluation under Rule 17(f)5 of the Investment Company Act and also issues a general exception to its requirements, thus permitting a customer to use non-U.S. banks as custodians of its foreign assets. This exception is issued however only provided that certain conditions are met. Known collectively as the Rule 17(f)5 Questions, they apply to and must be answered by U.S. registered mutual funds in respect of assets to be invested. Most custodians and their customers believe that the questions should be answered for all types of business. So what are the five questions?

1 Access

Whether applicable foreign law would restrict the access afforded to the company's independent public accountants to books and records kept by the eligible foreign custodian located in that country

2 Bankruptcy

Whether applicable foreign law would restrict the company's ability to recover assets in the event of the bankruptcy of the eligible foreign custodian based in that country

3 Loss

Whether applicable foreign law would restrict the company's ability to recover assets that are lost while under the control of an eligible foreign custodian located in that country

4 Expropriation

The likelihood of expropriation, nationalisation, freezes or confiscation of the company's assets

5 Convertibility

Whether difficulties in converting the company's cash and cash equivalents to U.S. Dollars are reasonably foreseeable

It is not difficult to see why, with other suitable questions, these five should be used for all types of assets.

As previously mentioned the SEC from June 2001 has somewhat eased the requirements for appointing a foreign custody provider. These requirements are governed by Rule 17(f)7 and include use of an Eligible Securities Depository and the relationship between the custodian and U.S. customer.

An **Eligible Securities Depository** is one that must:

1 Act or operate a system for the central handling of securities that is regulated by a foreign regulatory authority
2 Hold assets on behalf of the fund under safe-keeping conditions no less favourable than those that apply to other participants
3 Maintain records that identify the assets of participants, and keep its own assets separated from the assets of other participants
4 Provide periodic reports to participants
5 Undergo periodic examination by regulatory authorities or independent accountants

As far as the relationship is concerned, it is a question of analysing and monitoring the risk, including depository risk, and Rule 17(f) 7 requires the fund's contract with its primary (global) custodian to provide that the primary custodian will agree to exercise reasonable care, prudence and diligence in performing its duties under the rule, or adhere to a higher standard.

In the U.K. the complexities of what is deemed to be safeguarding and administration of another's assets and the relevant provisions, are ably explained in the Securities Institute IAQ Workbook entitled *Global Custody* and rather than repeat them here I would urge readers to avail themselves of the workbook if they need the detail.

Practical operations issues

What are the practical operations issues of complying with this internal and external regulation?

Perhaps the most obvious one, apart from not knowing the rules and regs anyway, is that where agreements are concerned over time the working processes covered by the agreement change.

For example, a custody agreement, client agreement, stock lending agreement and there are others, is set up at the beginning of the relationship or introduction of the service or facility. Highly important provisions concerning authorised personnel, etc. are contained in the agreements and must be complied with, and yet some months later there may be a change of personnel or growth of business that requires changes to the list of who for example, can authorise an asset movement by way of instruction to a custodian. In order to facilitate business the custodian and customers operations teams begin waiving the controls and procedures. This movement away from the agreed operating procedures must either be stopped or the procedures formally amended by agreement of the two parties.

One method of reducing the possibility of long term deviation away from agreed procedures is the regular audit process and another is spot checks instigated by operations managers.

A further operational consideration is the compliance with the money laundering regulations. Wherever there is client facing business there is a possibility of money launderers operating. Compliance with the initiatives and regulations designed to stop this activity is highly important and not just as far as a firm or organisation is concerned. There are implications too for the individuals. We look at money laundering in more detail in Chapter 5 but there are detailed regulations laid down relating to procedures and systems that must be in place and it is worth highlighting them here.

The procedures and systems that need to be put in place are required to:

- Deter money laundered from using a firm as a conduit for their illegal activities
- Identify and report suspicious transactions to the relevant law enforcement agency
- Keep an audit trail for use in any subsequent investigation into money laundering offences

In addition the Basle Supervisors Committee Statement of Principles on Money Laundering urged that there should be:

- Proper identification of all persons conducting business with the bank
- High ethical standards in bank business and compliance with laws and regulations governing financial transactions
- Co-operation with law enforcement authorities within the confines of applicable law
- Information and training for staff to ensure that they can carry out these principles

Money laundering is no minor issue being that it involves the proceeds of crime as well as terrorism. Colombian drug barons, criminal organisations, and 'Bin Ladens' alike need to launder their ill-gotten gains into 'clean' money, the latter two to finance their 'operations'. Every time such activity is recognised and action taken it is a blow struck for all the decent people in the world as well as for innocent victims of the low life.

The bottom line for operations people is simply report and record anything suspicious, however minor or irrelevant it may seem. Better to do that than end up in prison!

Time now to turn our attention to the retail markets and to look at how regulation works and what it means for operations teams involved in or servicing retail business.

Chapter 4

Client protection in the retail markets

In previous chapters I have referred to issues like Morgan Grenfell, pensions mis-selling and compliance with custody regulations. All of these are to a greater or lesser extent related to the retail market business.

Retail market business is everything from stocks and shares bought through a broker to mutual funds, insurance, pensions and finance products like credit cards, mortgages and loans.

In all cases someone is selling something to a client or investor either on an instruction basis or a discretionary basis. The products or services they sell can be an investment or a credit facility and the key thing is that the buyer should not, in any way, be abused, misled or subject to unnecessary or inappropriate risks. If this should happen then the regulator will want compensation paid to the investor and the perpetrator fined or banned or both.

Now you could argue that if this was enforced across the board there would be very little business going on as no one would take the risk of selling anything. This is a valid argument and the regulator does recognise that provided reasonable care and diligence is carried out by a party to a transaction with a customer, then a level of protection has been set which is fair to all.

The regulator sets some of this care and diligence requirement out whilst other standards are set as guidelines and the management of a firm is expected to manage its business accordingly. For instance the sale of some products requires a 'cooling-off period' so the customer can change their mind and firms that deal in products like derivatives should have clear procedures on accepting a customer for such products.

Client protection in the retail markets is really all about ensuring that the product the client obtains is reasonable for them, and that they have not been placed under pressure to purchase or sell a product or asset.

The 'hard sell' concept is one that most people will be familiar with. Whether it is time-share sales or the unsolicited phone call for double-glazing, people are put under unwanted pressure. There are also various other forms of selling, which are inappropriate, like those highlighted in the book *FIASCO* which was mentioned in the Preface. The concept of knowing your client is vital if the sales and marketing process is to be both successful and within the regulatory framework.

In the U.K. the FSA has, as we know, 11 Principles for Businesses and it is worth returning to the ones that are related to clients.

Principle 6: Customers' Interests
Requires a firm to pay due regard to the interests of its customers and treat them fairly

Principle 7: Communication with Clients
A firm must pay due regard to the information needs of its clients and communicate information to them in a way which is clear, fair and not misleading

Principle 8: Conflicts of Interest
A firm must manage conflicts of interest fairly, both between itself and a customer and between one customer and another client.

Principle 9: Customers: Relationship of Trust
A firm must take reasonable care to ensure the suitability of its advice and discretionary decisions for any customer who is entitled to rely on its judgement

Principle 10: Clients Assets

A firm must arrange adequate protection for clients' assets when it is responsible for them

These FSA Principles apply only to FSA regulated businesses and not to the unregulated business that a firm may undertake. The individual client must be aware that the level of protection for regulated and unregulated business is very different and therefore so too must the operations manager dealing with the retail business of a firm.

Retail business encompasses banking and investment and includes both standard products like mortgages and bank loans as well as 'packaged products' like units in regulated collective investment schemes. Interestingly, an Individual Savings Account (ISA) that might appear to be a packaged product is not in itself a packaged product, but the investments held in an ISA may well be packaged products and so are affected by the regulation.

Before going any further we need to understand the difference between the typical retail products on offer to the public. To do this we can look at three products common in the U.K., unit trusts, open-ended investment companies and investment trust companies.

Each of these products provides a means of investment and yet each is slightly different in its structure but not necessarily in terms of either the rewards or the risk that might accrue. For instance, a unit trust and an open-ended investment company(OEIC) might both invest in blue chip U.K. equities. To all intents and purposes there is no difference in the products in the risk or potential reward. If they are managed funds then the past track record of the fund manager is in general of more importance than whether the product is a unit trust or OEIC.

Table 4.1 is just a small example of the types of retail product available. To this we can add Individual Savings Accounts, life policies, off-shore funds, hedge funds, etc.

Table 4.1 Summary of the differences between unit trusts, OEICs and investment trusts

	Unit Trusts	**OEICs**	**Investment Trusts**
Status of Investors	Share in collective rights of assets Access to independent trustee	Investors are shareholders Rights are laid down in the regulations	Investors are shareholders in the investment trust Rights are laid down in the Companies Acts
Open/close ended	Open ended Units in existence rise or fall dependent on investors	Open ended Can redeem or issue shares on demand of investors	Close ended Fixed capital which can only be varied with permission of shareholders
Buying/Selling	Normally bought and sold through managers Bid/offer spread of approx. 5% Can be single priced	Bought or sold through Authorised Corporate Director (ACD) Single price but ACD may require payment of dilution levy	After launch they are bought and sold through brokers for a commission payment in the secondary market Price fixed by market
Price	Directly related to value of underlying portfolio and charges as laid down by regulator	Single price dependent on valuation of assets within fund	Dependent on market demand Shares usually trade at a discount to net asset value

Table 4.1 Continued

	Unit Trusts	**OEICs**	**Investment Trusts**
Securities within the trust/company	90% of portfolio must be held in authorized/ eligible stock markets	Invests in portfolio of shares and other securities	Wide range of securities can be purchased including unquoted and emerging market shares
Borrowing powers	Temporary, no longer than 3 months	Subject to any restrictions in instrument of incorporation No more than 10% of scheme property can be borrowed on any one day	Agreed in company's articles and may be increased by sanction of members
Management	Manager of trust with authority of trustee	ACD must be a corporation to provide for continuity	At least two directors
Meetings for investors	No requirement for regular meetings	Annual General Meeting Other meetings at directors calling	Annual General Meeting and as required under Companies Acts

With so much choice the investor often looks to the independent financial adviser (IFA) to assist them with their investment, insurance and retirement plans. The logic is simple enough; the investor gets advice from a qualified expert with access to all the various products available. However, we need to be careful here as some people are acting for a firm and so their 'independence' is not perhaps what it seems.

Polarisation

Of concern to the regulator is the fact that a person selling products or providing advice to a client needs to make clear whether they are acting for the firm or whether they are acting as an 'independent intermediary', and will give advice based on what is generally available in the market irrespective of the provider. Many Independent Financial Advisers (IFAs) are 'tied' to a firm. The term used is 'polarisation' and there are regulations known as the polarisation regime.

The problem is obvious. A tied representative is only advising and selling the provider firm's products. However there is no polarisation regime in respect of products sold without advice.

Suitability of products

The suitability of a product for a client is another key issue and as a result there are retail products where the investor has the right to a cooling-off period. Operations teams need to be aware of the client's rights and to ensure that the relevant cooling-off procedures are observed when dealing with these types of products.

Likewise, if a client is offered and use certain types of products, there may be documentation that must be provided that clearly sets out the terms and characteristics of the product.

Included in this area will be:

- Scheme Particulars
- Key Features
- Warrant and Derivatives Risk Warning

Two booklets, *The Morgan Stanley SICAV Brochure* (available in the following languages: English (United Kingdom), French, German,

Italian and Spanish) and *Key Features of the Morgan Stanley SICAV* (available in English), provide a broad and informative overview of Morgan Stanley Fund offerings. These publications can be downloaded from:

http://sicav.msdw.com/hamilton/public/ publications.html

The brochures are examples of the content of typical Scheme Particulars and Key Features documents that apply to mutual funds and unit trusts (the reader can compare documents from different companies either by study offers sent through the mail or alternatively accessing the websites of leading providers of these products such as Morgan Stanley from where these examples were taken, M&G, AXA, Standard Life Investments, etc.).

This documentation is in addition to any Terms and Conditions that apply to the business being transacted with and for the customer.

Record keeping

The maintenance of proper and accurate records is also a primary role of operations and this is also crucially important in terms of dealing with clients. Amongst the data that must be maintained is:

- Client's name and address
- Approval/rejection of use of Client data
- Client activity
- Client complaints
- All correspondence

The FSA Conduct of Business Rules require that where an aggregated transaction, i.e. one where several individual client orders are transacted together, takes place, the firm must record the identity of each client involved. Where there are such multiple orders the firm must record the basis of allocation if, for instance, the total order is not completed as soon as is practical which allows a firm to establish the basis after the transaction. This is necessary for practical operational reasons. Should an aggregate order contain orders for the firm and customers, then the firm must record the basis of allocation before the transaction takes place.

The following must be recorded:

- Date and time of allocation
- The designated investment involved
- Identity of each party involved
- Amount allocated to each party

Such records must be kept for three years from the date of allocation.

Other areas where records are required include where loans are made, and this will include recording the basis on which the conclusions about the client's financial standing were made and also

Table 4.2

	Order Received	Discretionary Decision	Order Executed
Name of Customer	Yes	Yes	Yes
Date/Time	On Receipt	At decision to deal	When deal is done
Employee ID	Who received the order	Who decided to deal	Who undertook the transaction
Instrument	Yes	Yes	Yes
Buy/Sell	Yes	Yes	Yes
Quantity	Including price and limit	Quantity	Quantity
Instructions	Received by fax/ phone, etc.	N/A	N/A
Counterparty	N/A	N/A	Yes (if known)
Principal Trade	N/A	N/A	Yes

Source: The Securities Institute, FSA Regulatory Environment IAQ Workbook

customer execution records. Table 4.2 shows the summarised requirements.

Reporting to clients

There are rules in all jurisdictions related to reporting to customers. One obvious reason that regulators are concerned that this is done efficiently and in a timely manner, is that a customer must be able to reconcile the purchase or sale of a product or instrument made on their behalf.

Therefore there are requirements related to providing confirmation of the order completed and in many cases this is no later than the next business day following the transaction. It is also often a requirement that this is in written form, which includes electronically, and whilst this may be provided today via posting the confirmation on a secure part of the firms website, the firm must have a means to see that the client has actually viewed the confirmation.

Under the FSA Rules in the U.K., in some circumstances a client can elect not to receive such confirmation and other exceptions are permitted related to life policies, personal pensions and series of payments for instruments when again no confirmation is sent.

Periodic statements

Firms acting for customers where the firm holds investments and assets on behalf of the customers, as for instance a fund manager does, need to provide periodic information about the assets currently held, movements in holdings and values, etc. to the customers.

The extent of the data and the frequency of provision of the data are determined by both a regulatory requirement and a commercial one, i.e. when and how does the client want the information?

The regulatory requirement varies as to both frequency and content but in most cases such statements will need to be sent at least once a year, maybe more frequently, and the records of the statements must in the U.K. be kept for three years.

Other regulation that protects customers

The level of protection afforded to customers does vary from country to country and the scope of this book means we can only take a look at a very small sample. The operations team member would benefit enormously by researching the primary rules and regulation providing protection to clients in the leading markets and this can be done by accessing the websites of the major regulators (see the Morgan Stanley brochures mentioned previously).

Most regulation in retail markets relates to selling and protecting the customer's assets and so we have client money rules and disclosure rules related to charges, commissions, etc. as well as many rules that relate to advertising, cold-calling, cooling-off periods, etc.

Today we also have the requirement to ensure that products are suitable for the customer's investment profile and that the customer understands the risk involved in their investments. Hence, we have the Warrants and Derivatives Risk Warning document covered earlier in the chapter.

To protect the client and the firm the customer deals with, there is often a need to have a customer sign a formal Terms of Business and Customer Agreement that sets out the various issues that can apply to investments and the product, and that the customer acknowledges this by signing the Agreement.

Remember of course that the regulation and therefore level of protection afforded to a client varies depending on the classification of the client and the type of product. It goes without saying that the records of why a client was classified as 'Private' and what was transacted for that client must be maintained along with, of course, details of any complaint that the customer may have made and any resolution of the problem.

Chapter 5

Money laundering

Money Laundering is something that all regulators are concerned with. Given that in 2001 banks in the U.K. reported over 31,000 suspicious transactions to the National Criminal Intelligence Service and that there is likely to be a doubling of that figure in 2002, the concern is well placed.

So how is the industry seeking to deal with money laundering?

The Financial Action Task Force (FATF) published a report containing Forty Recommendations, which are generally recognised as the blueprint for international action against money laundering.

The FATF is a body made up of regulators from a number of countries. These regulators, including representatives from European countries are concerned about ensuring the integrity of the international financial system, including prevention of money laundering.

Its meetings cover not only monitoring of members' compliance with the recommendations, but also monitoring developments and examining counter-measures and promoting world-wide action against money laundering.

Money laundering can be described as:

"The process by which criminals attempt to conceal the true origin and ownership of the proceeds of their criminal activities."

This is achieved by introducing the proceeds of crime, such as drug dealing, into the mainstream of financial activities which results in them being legitimised. Therefore firms must have procedures for identifying suspicious transactions and for confirming the identity of new clients. In addition firms must establish training programmes for staff and advise them of their personal responsibility to report suspicious events. These must in turn be reported to the regulatory authorities.

The 1993 Money Laundering Regulations are aimed at:

- Banks and building societies
- Insurance companies
- Firms carrying out investment business under the FSA

The reason is simple enough. Money laundering makes use of the financial markets in many ways. Bank accounts, money transfers, processes associated with types of investment and specific products, cross-border activity, insurance policies, etc.

The regulations require firms to:

- Appoint a Money Laundering Reporting Officer to whom suspicious transactions will be reported
- Have "know your customer" procedures
- Establish procedures to monitor transactions and identify suspicious ones
- Establish reporting procedures
- Have in place adequate control systems
- Have proper record keeping procedures
- Ensure complete training of all personnel

A failure to implement the regulations is imprisonment and or fines applicable to both individuals and firms. Tough measures you may think but the issue of money laundering, involving as it does the proceeds from terrorism, drug dealing and organised and often violent crime, is a very serious one for all countries and every citizen. As the money launderer needs either inside help from banks, brokers and other organisations or alternatively if they can take advantage of weak controls, the roles of both individuals and firms in preventing and reporting suspicions of money laundering are key to successfully defeating the criminals.

How does money laundering take place?

Within the capital markets there are many products that utilise cash movements either frequently, like derivatives, or in large amounts like bond and FX transactions.

The following is an example of how a money launderer might successfully launder their illegal money utilising the derivatives market.

Facts
The following typology is provided as an example of how funds could be laundered using the derivatives market.

In this method, the broker must be willing to allocate genuinely losing trades to the account in which criminal proceeds are deposited. Instead of relying on misleading or false documentation, the broker uses the genuine loss making documentation to be allocated to the detriment of the dirty money account holder. As an example, a broker uses two accounts, one called 'A' into which the client regularly deposits money which needs laundering, and one called 'B' which is intended to receive the laundered funds. The broker enters the trading market and 'goes long' (purchases) 100 derivative contracts of a commodity, trading at an offer price of $85.02, with a 'tick' size of $25. At the same time he 'goes short' (sells) 100 contracts of the same commodity at the bid price of $85.00. At that moment, he has two legitimate contracts which have been cleared through the floor of the exchange.

Later in the trading day, the contract price has altered to $84.72 bid and $84.74 offered. The broker returns to the market, closing both open positions at the prevailing prices. Now, the broker, in his own books assigns the original purchase at $85.02 and the subsequent sale at $84.72 to account A. The percentage difference between the two prices is 30 points or ticks (the difference between $84.72 and $85.02). To calculate the loss on this contract, the tick size which is $25 is multiplied by the number of contracts, 100, multiplied by the price movement, 30. Thus: $25 × 100 × 30 = $75,000 (loss).

The other trades are allocated to the B account, which following the same calculation theory of tick size multiplied by the number of contracts multiplied by the price movement results in a profit as follows: $25 × 100 × 26 = $65,000 (profit).

The account containing the money to be laundered has just paid out $75,000 for the privilege of receiving a profit of $65,000 on the other side.

In other words, the launderer has paid $10,000 for the privilege of successfully laundering $75,000. Such a sum is well within the amount of premium which professional launderers are prepared to pay for the privilege of cleaning up such money. As a transaction, it is perfectly lawful from the point of view of the broker. He has not taken the risk of creating false documentation, which could conceivably be discovered, and everything has been done in full sight of the market.

Source: JMLSG Money Laundering Guidance Notes

Another example of money laundering is cross border cash. Consider the following case:

Facts

Three suspicious transaction reports were received relating to a number of transactions which were carried out at Danish banks whereby large amounts of money were deposited into accounts and then withdrawn shortly afterwards as cash. The first report was received in August 1994, and concerned an account held by a Mr. X. Upon initial investigation, the subjects of the reports (X,Y and Z) were not known in police databases as being connected to drugs or any other criminal activity. However further investigation showed that X had imported more than 3 tonnes of hashish into Denmark over a 9 year period. Y had assisted him on one occasion, whilst Z had assisted in laundering the money.

Most of the money was transported by Z as cash from Denmark to Luxembourg where X and Z held 16 accounts at different banks, or to Spain and subsequently Gibraltar, where they held 25 accounts. The receipts from the Danish banks for the withdrawn money were used as documentation to prove the legal origin of the money, when the money was deposited into banks in Gibraltar and Luxembourg.

It turned out that sometimes the same receipt was used at several banks so that more cash could be deposited as "legal" than had actually been through the Danish bank accounts.

Results
X and Y were arrested, prosecuted and convicted for drug trafficking offences and received sentences of six and two years imprisonment respectively. A confiscation order for the equivalent of U.S.$ 6 million was made against X. Z was convicted of drug money laundering involving U.S.$ 1.3 million, and was sentenced to one year nine months imprisonment.

Lessons
Financial institutions should not accept proof of deposit to a bank account as being equivalent to proof of a legitimate origin.

Carrying illegal proceeds as cash across national borders remains an important method of money laundering.

Source: JMLSG Money Laundering Guidance Note

These two examples are taken from the excellent Guidance Notes for The Financial Sector published by the Joint Money Laundering Steering Group. Another useful illustration obtainable from the same source is that of the contents of the Money Laundering Reporting Officers (MLRO) Annual Report.

As part of the controls and procedures that the regulations require firms to have in place to combat money laundering is the appointment of an MLRO.

The following information has been sourced from the JMLSG Guidance Notes and the reference number is provided for readers who might wish to study the subject in more detail.

The MLRO's Annual Report

3.15. FSA requirements for Senior Management Arrangements, Systems and Controls – SYC 3.2.6R requires a firm to take reasonable care to establish and maintain adequate systems and controls for compliance with its regulatory obligations and to counter the risk that it might be used to further financial crime. In recognition of this requirement, FSA Evidential Provision 7.2.2 within the money laundering sourcebook states that arrangements must include requirements that:

a at least once in each calendar year the relevant firm commission a report from its MLRO which:
  - i assesses the relevant firm's compliance with the money laundering sourcebook;
  - ii indicates, in particular, the way in which new findings on countries with anti-money laundering inadequacies have been used during the year; and
  - iii gives the number of internal reports made by staff, dealing separately, if appropriate, with different parts of the relevant firm's business;

b the relevant firm's senior management considers the report; and

c they take any necessary action to remedy deficiencies identified by the report.

3.16. FSA Guidance 7.2.3 states that figures for internal reports should be broken down, if appropriate, in the MLRO's report.

Firms will need to use their judgement as to how the MLRO should be required to break down the figures in order to achieve this aim. FSA Guidance 7.2.3 states that the purpose of the report is to enable a relevant firm's senior management to assess whether internal reports are being made whenever required and that an overall figure which seems satisfactory does not conceal inadequate reporting in a particular part of the relevant firm's business.

3.17. It is suggested, by way of example, that the annual report might cover information of the following nature:

- any changes made or recommended in respect of new legislation, rules or industry guidance;
- serious compliance deficiencies that have been identified relating to current policies and procedures, indicating the seriousness of the issue, and either the action taken or recommendations for change;
- a risk assessment of any new types of products and services, or any new channels for distributing them, and the money laundering compliance measures that have either been implemented or are recommended;
- the nature of the actions taken following the publication of findings concerning a non co-operative jurisdiction, the results of that review and the measures taken to monitor business with that jurisdiction;
- the number of internal reports that have been received from each separate division, product area, subsidiary, etc.;
- the percentage of those reports that have been submitted to NCIS;
- any perceived deficiencies in the reporting procedures and any changes implemented or recommended;
- information concerning which staff have received training during the period the method of training and any significant key issues arising out of the training;
- any additional information concerning communications to staff; and
- any recommendations concerning additional resource requirements to ensure effective compliance.

3.18. Larger groups might choose to prepare a single report covering all of its authorised firms, provided that, within the report, there are separate sections covering the requirements for each authorised firm.

3.19. To assist the MLRO in preparing the annual report, and to ensure that the MLRO annual report is a fair and accurate assessment, firms are recommended to make arrangements to verify, on a regular basis,

> compliance with policies, procedures, and controls relating to money laundering activities. Firms may wish to ask their internal audit or compliance department, as appropriate, to undertake this role, or seek an assessment from external sources.
>
> **3.20.** It is important that the procedures and responsibilities for monitoring compliance with and effectiveness of money laundering policies and procedures are clearly laid down by all firms and communicated to management and staff.

Practical operational considerations

We have seen how money laundering is an extensive problem in the industry and that there is a regulation designed to help prevent such activity. From the examples given, anyone working in an operations environment can see how the involvement of operations, albeit one hopes not direct involvement, occurs.

What then are the practical issues that arise in money laundering?

Firstly a key element in combating is quite simply:

KNOW YOUR CUSTOMER AND IDENTIFICATION EVIDENCE

Having sufficient information about your customer and making use of that information underpins all other anti-money laundering procedures and is the most effective weapon against being used to launder the proceeds of crime. In addition to minimising the risk of being used for illicit activities, it provides protection against fraud, enables suspicious activity to be recognised, and protects individual firms from reputational and financial risks.

In general terms one would expect a firm to never establish a business relationship until all relevant parties to the relationship have been identified and the nature of the business they expect to conduct has been established. Once an on-going business relationship has been established, any regular business undertaken for that customer should be assessed against the expected pattern of activity of the customer.

Any unexplained activity can then be examined to determine whether there is a suspicion of money laundering. Of course this kind of active monitoring of the relationship with a customer is likely to be occurring as part of risk management anyway.

It is important to recognise that the customer identification process does not start and end at the point of application.

The process of confirming and updating identity, address and any other relevant data on the customer is an on-going process.

The extent and type of additional KYC information collected will differ from sector to sector and between firms within any sector. It will also depend on the nature of the product or service being offered and whether personal contact is maintained enabling file notes of discussion to be made or whether all contact with the customer is remote. In the retail markets where so much activity is via the Internet there may be no personal contact whatsoever with the end client.

How then does a firm identify a customer?

Let us look at the Guidance Notes issued by the JMLSG. (the Guidance Note reference is given for readers who wish to obtain the Guidance Notes for further study).

Identity

Identity generally means a set of attributes which together uniquely identify a natural or legal person. For example, an individual's identity comprises his/her name including all other names used; and the residential address at which s/he can be located.

4.21. Date of birth is also important as an identifier in support of the name and is essential to law enforcement agencies in an investigation. In addition, obtaining a date of birth provides an extra safeguard if, for example, a forged or stolen passport or driving licence is used to confirm identity which bears a date of birth that is clearly inconsistent with the age of the person presenting the document. *However, there is no requirement to verify the date of birth provided.*

4.22. Information concerning residency and/or nationality is also useful in assessing whether a customer is resident in a high-risk country. Both residency and nationality can also be necessary, in a non-money laundering context, for preventing breaches of UN or other international sanctions to which the U.K. may be a party from time to time. Consequently, where a passport is taken as evidence of identity, the number, date and country of issue should be recorded. Firms operating in U.S.$ markets will also need to take account of the U.S. OFAC requirements and the necessity to 'interdict' funds transfers to/from OFAC listed countries and individuals.

When must identity be verified

4.23. Whenever a business relationship is to be established, e.g. when an account is to be opened, or a significant one-off transaction or series of linked transactions is undertaken, identification evidence must be obtained.

4.24. FSA Guidance 3.1.2 explains that, subject to certain exemptions, "transaction" in this sourcebook, includes the giving of advice, and thus has a wide meaning throughout this sourcebook.

4.25. Once identification procedures have been satisfactorily completed, and the business relationship has been established, *as long as contact or activity is maintained and records concerning that customer are kept in accordance with Section 7*, no further evidence of identity is needed when transactions or activity are subsequently undertaken.

Redemptions/Surrenders

4.26. When an investor finally cashes in his investment (wholly or partially), if the amount payable is Euro 15,000 or more, then his/her identity must be verified and recorded if it has not been done previously. This requirement will not apply where the original investment was made prior to 1 April 1994 (the date when the Regulations took effect), except where the registered holder to whom the payment is to be made was not a registered holder at 1 April 1994, irrespective of how the transfer or change of beneficial interest arose.

4.27. In the case of a redemption or surrender of an investment (wholly or partially), a firm will be considered to have taken reasonable measures to establish the identity of the investor where payment is made:

- to the legal owner of the investment by means of a cheque crossed "account payee"; or
- to a bank account held (solely or jointly) in the name of the legal owner of the investment by any electronic means effective to transfer funds.

Whose identity should be verified

4.28. FSA Rule 3.1.3 states that

1 A relevant firm must take steps to find out who its client is by obtaining sufficient evidence of the identity of any client who comes into contact with the firm to be able to show that the client is who he claims to be.
2 Where the client with whom the relevant firm has contact is, or appears to be, acting on behalf of another, the obligation is to obtain sufficient evidence of both their identities
3 This Rule is subject to the exceptions

4.29. FSA Guidance 3.1.1 advises that there are special provisions in Chapter 3 for cases where the person with whom the relevant firm has contact is acting for another. Broadly, the relevant firm has to enquire into the identity of both persons, unless a relevant exemption enables it to focus solely on the person it is actually in contact with. However, in accordance with Regulation 10(1)(b) and FSA Rule 3.2.2(1), the obligation to identify does not apply if the client, i.e. the applicant for business, is also a U.K. or EU credit or financial institution

4.30. Consequently:

- where a firm believes that its client is acting on its own account (rather than for a specific client or group of clients); and
- where the client is a bank, broker, fund manager or other regulated firm; and
- where all business is to be undertaken in the name of the firm, there is no obligation to look beyond the client.

4.31. In other circumstances, unless the client is another regulated firm acting as agent on behalf of one or more underlying clients from within the U.K. or EU, or from a non-EU country and has given written assurance that he has obtained and recorded evidence of identity at least to the standards required by the European Directive identification evidence should usually be verified for:

- the named account holder(s)/the person in whose name an investment is registered;
- any principal beneficial owner of funds being invested who is not the account holder or named investor, i.e. normally those with 20% interest or more (see paragraph 4.163);
- the principal controller(s) of an account or business relationship, i.e. those who regularly provide instructions; and
- any intermediate parties, e.g. where an account is managed or owned by an intermediary.

Taking a risk-based approach, firms should also consider whether it would be appropriate to identify directors who are not principal controllers and/or some of the signatories to an account.

4.32. In respect of joint applicants, identification evidence should be obtained for all account holders, not only the first named. However, in the case of applicants who have the same surname and address (normally husband and wife), the name and address of the first named should be verified but only the name need be verified in the case of the second applicant. For example, in these circumstances, the same document or electronic check can be used to verify the address of both account holders if both applicants are named on the verification record.

4.33. Subject to paragraphs 4.12–4.13, it is important that for higher risk business undertaken for private companies, i.e. those not listed on a recognised stock exchange, sufficient evidence of identity and address is verified for:

- the principal underlying beneficial owner(s) of the company, i.e. normally those with 20% interest or more; and
- those with principal control over the company's assets, e.g. principal controllers/directors or shadow directors.

Firms should be alert for circumstances that might indicate any significant changes in the nature of the business or its ownership and make enquiries accordingly.

4.34. In respect of trusts, the identity of those providing funds, i.e. the settlor(s) and those who are authorised to invest or transfer funds, or to make decisions on behalf of the trust, i.e. the principal trustees and any controllers who have the power to remove the trustees, should be verified.

Regular Savings Schemes and Savings Accounts – Investments in the Name of Third Parties

4.35. When an investor sets up a savings account or a regular savings scheme, whereby the funds are supplied by one person for investment in the name of another (such as a spouse or a child), the person who funds the subscription or makes deposits into the savings scheme should be regarded as the applicant for business for whom identification evidence must be obtained in addition to the legal owner. (It should be noted that law enforcement evidence suggests that child/spouse accounts are frequently used for illegal purposes).

Personal Pension Schemes

4.36. Unless personal pensions are connected to a policy of insurance and taken out by virtue of a contract of employment or pension scheme, they are not exempt under the Money Laundering Regulations, or consequently the FSA Rules, and identification evidence must be obtained at the outset for all investors. A number of different pension scheme scenarios, and the relevant identification procedures, are set out in Annex 1, Section 4.

4.37. Personal pensions advisers who are covered by the Regulations can be relied upon to confirm that identity has been taken; those who are not covered by the Regulations should be charged with obtaining the identification evidence on behalf of the pension fund provider. Confirmation that identification evidence has been taken should be given on the transfer of a pension to another provider.

Timing of identification requirements

4.38. Regulation 11 states that what constitutes an acceptable time span for obtaining satisfactory evidence of identity must be determined in the light of all the circumstances. This will include the nature of the business, the geographical location of the parties and whether it is practical to obtain the evidence before commitments are entered into or money changes hands.

However, any occasion when business is conducted before satisfactory evidence of identity has been obtained must be in

exceptional circumstances only and those circumstances justified with regard to the risk.

4.39. FSA Rule 3.1.8. clarifies this by stating that

1 A relevant firm must obtain identification evidence as soon as reasonably practicable after it has contact with a client with a view to:
   a agreeing with the client to carry out an initial transaction; or
   b reaching an understanding (whether binding or not) with the client that it may carry out future transactions;
2 If the client does not supply identification evidence within the time scale in (1), the relevant firm must:
   a discontinue any regulated activity it is conducting for him; and
   b bring to an end any understanding it has reached with him;

   unless, in either case, the relevant firm has informed the National Criminal Intelligence Service (NCIS).

4.40. FSA Rule 3.1.9 advises that nothing in 3.1.8(2) requires a relevant firm to continue with a transaction which conflicts with its obligations, if any, in relation to the rights of a third party.

4.41. As stated previously, FSA Guidance 3.1.2 advises that "transaction" includes the giving of advice. Advice is not, however, intended to apply to the provision of information about the availability of products or services or to apply to a first interview/discussion prior to a relationship being established.

4.42. To comply with the Regulations and the FSA Rules, a firm may start processing the business or application immediately, provided that it:

- promptly takes appropriate steps to obtain identification evidence; and
- does not transfer or pay any money out to a third party until the identification requirements have been satisfied.

4.43. The failure or refusal by an applicant to provide satisfactory identification evidence within a reasonable timeframe and without adequate explanation may lead to a suspicion that the depositor or investor is engaged in money laundering. In such circumstances, firms should consider making a suspicion report to NCIS based on the information in their possession and, following this, should obtain NCIS consent ***before any funds are returned to where they came from***.

4.44. In preparing their procedures, firms will need to establish clear and consistent policies to deal with situations where satisfactory evidence of identity cannot be obtained and, if necessary, close the account or unwind the transactions.

Cancellation/Cooling Off

4.45. Where an investor exercises cancellation rights or cooling-off rights, the sum invested must be re-paid (subject to any shortfall deduction where applicable). However this could offer a readily available route for laundering money, and intermediaries and product providers should therefore be alert to any abnormal exercise of cancellation/cooling-off rights by any investor, or in respect of business introduced through any single authorised intermediary.

In the event that abnormal exercise of these rights becomes apparent, the matter should be treated as suspicious and reported through the usual channels.

IDENTIFICATION PROCEDURES: GENERAL PRINCIPLES

4.46. A firm should establish to its satisfaction that it is dealing with a real person or organisation (natural, corporate or legal), and obtain identification evidence sufficient to establish that the applicant is that person or organisation. When reliance is being placed on any third party to identify or confirm the identity of any applicant, the overall legal responsibility to ensure that the procedures and evidence obtained are satisfactory rests with the account holding firm.

4.47. The requirement in all cases is to obtain satisfactory evidence that a person of that name lives at the address given and that the applicant is that person, or that the company has identifiable owners and that its representatives can be located at the address provided.

4.48. **Because no single form of identification can be fully guaranteed as genuine, or representing correct identity, the identification process will need to be cumulative. Unless the applicant falls within the definition of "financial exclusion", no single document or source of data (except for a database constructed from a number of other reliable data sources) must therefore be used to verify both name and permanent address.**

4.49. It is important that the procedures adopted to verify the identity of private individuals are sufficiently robust whether the procedures are being undertaken face to face or remotely. Reasonable steps should be taken to avoid single or multiple fictitious applications or substitution (impersonation) fraud for the purpose of money laundering.

4.50. Other than in financial exclusion cases, an introduction from a respected customer personally known to a Director or Manager, or an introduction from a member of staff, will often provide comfort **but must not replace the need for identification evidence set out in paragraphs 4.72–4.100** (readers will need to obtain a copy of the Guidance Notes). Details of who initiated and authorised the introduction should be kept with the customer's account opening records. Directors/Senior Managers must not require or request other staff to waive normal identification procedures as a favour to the applicant.

New business for existing customers

4.51. When an existing customer closes one account and opens another, or enters into a new agreement to purchase products or services, there is no need to reverify identity or address unless the name or the address provided do not match the firm's records. However, procedures should exist to guard against impersonation fraud and the opportunity should also be taken to ask the customer to confirm the relevant details and obtain any missing KYC information. This is particularly important:

- if there was an existing business relationship with the customer as at 1 April 1994 (i.e. the date when the Regulations took effect) and identification evidence has not previously been obtained; or
- if there has been no recent contact or correspondence with the customer, e.g. within the past twelve months; or
- when a previously dormant account is re-activated.

4.52. In the circumstances set out in paragraph 4.51 above, details of the previous account(s) and any identification evidence previously obtained, or any introduction records, should be linked to the new account records and retained for the relevant period in accordance with the guidance set out in Section 7.

Certification of identification documents

4.53. To guard against the dangers of postal intercept and fraud, prospective customers should not be asked to send originals of valuable personal identity documents, e.g. passport, identity card, driving licence, etc. by post.

4.54. In the event that internal procedures require documentary evidence where there is no face to face contact, then copies certified by a U.K. lawyer, banker, authorised financial intermediary, MCCB regulated mortgage broker, accountant, teacher, doctor, minister of religion or post master/sub-post master should be requested. The person undertaking the certification must be capable of being contacted if necessary.

4.55. In the case of a passport, national identity card or documentary evidence of address for a non U.K. national, the copy can be certified by:

- an embassy, consulate or high commission of the country of issue; or
- by a senior official within the account opening firm or group; or
- by a lawyer or attorney.

4.56. Certified copies of identification evidence should be dated, and signed "original seen." In situations where a good reproduction of photographic evidence of identity cannot be achieved, the copy should be certified as providing a good likeness of the applicant.

Records of identification evidence

4.57. The Regulations and FSA Rules require that records of the supporting evidence and methods used to verify identity must be retained for five years after the account is closed or the business relationship ended, in line with the guidance given in Section 7- Record Keeping.

4.58. File copies of the supporting documentary evidence of identity must be retained for the statutory period set out in paragraph 4.57 above. Where the supporting evidence could not be copied at the time it was obtained, the reference numbers and other relevant details of the identification evidence obtained should be recorded to enable the documents to be re-obtained. Confirmation should be provided that the original documents were seen by certifying either on the photocopies themselves or on the record of the evidence provided.

4.59. Where checks are made electronically, a record of the actual information obtained, or a record of where it can be re-obtained, must be retained as part of the identification evidence. The requirement is to be able to reproduce the actual information that would have been obtained at the time.

The above extracts from the Guidance Notes are designed to give the reader, particularly those working in an operations environment a concept of what is required in the areas of money laundering generally and in 'know your client' specifically. I would stress however that the reader should visit the websites of the JMLSG and the British Bankers Association and where applicable obtain a copy of the Guidance Notes for their own use.

Summary

OK, so now we should be in no doubt as to the importance of money laundering and the need to have adequate procedures in place that will cover issues like

- Know your customer
- Know who your MLRO is
- Procedures to identify clients
- Procedures to identify suspicious transactions
- Escalation procedures
- Adequate records for audit trail

Time then to look at another couple of unsavoury aspects of the financial markets that regulators seek to deal with, namely fraud and insider dealing.

Before we do so however we should just remind ourselves of how serious a situation involving money laundering is by looking at the penalties for criminal offences associated with money laundering in the U.K.

Penalties for:

Assistance: provision of assistance to a money launderer to obtain, conceal, retain or invest funds if that person knows or suspects that those funds are the proceeds of serious criminal conduct

Maximum 14 years in prison and/or an unlimited fine

Tipping Off: anyone who prejudices an investigation by informing the person who is subject of suspicion, or any third party, that a disclosure has been made or that the authorities are liable to act

Maximum 5 years in prison and/or an unlimited fine

Failure To Report: in the cases of drug trafficking and terrorist activity only it is an offence not to report knowledge or suspicions as soon as possible

Maximum 5 years in prison and/or unlimited fine

It is also worth noting that in December 2002 the second largest bank in the U.K. was fined £750,000 by the FSA for having "inadequate" money laundering controls

Operations managers and personnel beware!!

Chapter 6

Fraud and insider dealing

Fraud and insider dealing; there is nothing the popular press like more than a juicy story about the 'dodgy' dealing and criminal activity of those employed in the financial markets and to be fair there has been plenty of stories for them to get the headlines to blaze across the front page.

WorldCom, Enron, Maxwell, Leeson, the 'Flaming Ferraris', the list goes on, for despite the best efforts of and the increasing powers given to the regulators in most jurisdictions, there is always going to be the opportunity and someone clever enough to exploit it.

In some respects fraud is accepted as part of the 'risk' of the financial markets and some would say that the victims of fraud deserve it because they should have been aware of what was going on. I would counter that argument by saying that it may be true that the senior managers (assuming they are not involved in the fraud!!) should be able to make a reasonable attempt to prevent it occurring, but usually the impact of the fraud will have far reaching consequences and affect many who are vulnerable, and therefore not in a position to be aware of what is going on, the Mirror Group pensioners being a prime example.

Fraud is a criminal act and yet we have to differentiate between the 'petty' fraud, i.e. the unauthorised personal telephone call at the employers expense and the more serious fraud that affects possibly many thousands of people. When Enron collapsed, or WorldCom 'inflated' their profits, hundreds of thousands of investors who had investments that held the stock of those companies lost out badly, many millions more were affected by the global fall in share prices because of reaction to the events. Yet the people at the top of both companies, who have at least some responsibility for what happened will be in a far better position, given their personal wealth, to overcome the problem they have been instrumental in creating than most others. It is a massive moral issue and one that regulators and politicians have to address if financial markets are not to suffer a massive vote of no confidence by investors.

For the operations manager fraud and insider dealing are two quite different issues. The process of settlement will be contributing to the control over insider dealing through the production of data on trades, settlement, etc. but the operations team will, in all probability, not be aware of a potential insider deal. In fact the discovery of insider activity usually only occurs once an event or announcement affecting the company's share price has occurred. Client activity in the relevant shares may then become subject to investigation. Slightly different is the situation where the company that employs the operations personnel is itself a quoted company. Here, there is a distinct possibility that some employees will have access to information regarding the profitability or otherwise of the firm, performance comparisons and future business plans. Even when the employees are only seeing part of the process or snippets of the financial information related to the firm, they may be able to judge or hear reasonably accurate 'rumours', often related to bonuses, which enable them to have 'inside', i.e. privileged information that may affect the share price that is not available publicly and therefore they have the potential to benefit from it.

As a consequence, firms have a strict set of rules relating to staff dealing in both the company's shares and options if applicable and also in securities in general, particularly those that the firm deals in or has a corporate finance relationship with. This will often relate to restrictions and or embargos on dealing but can include total prohibition of any activity. These conditions may apply also to close relatives of the individual employee.

The operations team are obviously included in any staff dealing rules and also may be part of the process of administering the controls. They are also very much involved in the process of monitoring and reconciling the positions relating to assets both cash and securities.

Fraud in the financial markets is more widespread than people probably imagine. In a sense this is not surprising as few firms would want to publicise that they have been the victims of fraud, it hardly induces confidence in their ability to manage risk!

Fraud is occurring in terms of the illegal use and theft of assets and manipulating data to make gain where gain would not otherwise have happened, i.e. the inflating of dealing profits, sales commission, hiding losses, etc. that then result in bonus or commission payments. How does this happen when we have increasing use of electronic book entry settlement and immobilised securities rather than physical evidence of ownership?

The answer is that false instructions to credit and debit accounts or move assets are made and so we have a twin track problem, physical theft and electronic theft. Of course theft is not always occurring in the way in which we assume theft happens, i.e. the total and often irrecoverable removal of the asset. Sometimes the theft can be in the form of the illegal 'borrowing' of assets.

The following are some illustrations of what can happen and how the U.K. regulator dealt with it:

19 February 2001

GRIFFIN: 'ROGUE' TRADER EXPELLED BY REGULATOR

The Securities and Futures Authority has expelled a registered trader who undertook unauthorised (or 'rogue') trades, two firms through which he operated, and the senior managers who failed to control his trading. The scale of the trader's unauthorised business brought down derivatives firm Griffin Trading Company in December 1998.

Mr John Ho Park was a trader with a firm called GLH (Derivatives) Limited that traded using facilities provided by Griffin, a U.K. branch of a U.S. company. Mr Park took out such large positions in the Eurex futures market on 21 and 22 December 1998 that neither he, GLH nor Griffin could meet the obligations he created. Griffin and GLH have since ceased to carry on investment business. Griffin subsequently went into liquidation.

The regulator found that on several occasions between July and December 1998, Mr Park had deliberately and substantially exceeded the limits within which he was allowed to trade. Management were unaware of most of Mr Park's trading limits breaches and were misled by Mr Park about the extent of his trading activities. On one occasion (in July 1998) some of the management did become aware that Park had breached his trading limits but they did not take steps to prevent further breaches.

Because of his failure to observe high standards of integrity and fair dealing, Mr Park has been found not fit and proper to be registered with SFA in any capacity.

Mr Scott Szach, based in the United States, was Senior Executive Officer of Griffin (U.K. branch), responsible for Griffin's management and control and its risk management. In addition to failing to implement adequate controls over the company, he also conducted unauthorised trading for much of 1998 and deliberately sought to conceal his trading from Griffin's senior management by making fictitious entries in Griffin's books and records. By 23 December 1998, the losses he had incurred totalled approximately U.S.$2 million. He was judged not fit and proper to be registered with SFA in any capacity and has been expelled. In January 2001, the U.S. Commodity Futures Trading Commission (CFTC) settled proceedings against Mr Szach concerning his role in Griffin, including banning him from trading for ten years.

Mr Steven Rose, Griffin's Compliance Officer, was responsible for compliance matters at Griffin, which included risk management. For failing to act with due skill, care and diligence, he has been expelled as no longer fit and proper to be registered with SFA as a Compliance Officer and has also been suspended from the SFA Register of Managers. Mr

Darren Lee was Senior Executive Officer of GLH and, as such, was responsible for GLH's management and control and its risk management. He has been expelled as no longer fit and proper to be registered with SFA as a Senior Executive Officer or as a Director.

As Compliance Officer of GLH, Mr Richard Gilbert was responsible for compliance matters at GLH, including risk management. He has been expelled as no longer fit and proper to be registered with SFA as a Compliance Officer and has been suspended from the SFA Register of Directors.

Both Griffin and GLH have been expelled from SFA.

Source: Financial Services Authority

Note

1 SFA is the regulatory organisation established under the Financial Services Act 1986 with responsibility for regulating members of all the organised City investment markets, i.e. the stock market, eurobond, financial futures, commodity futures markets and also corporate finance specialists and off-market traders. Around 1,350 firms are regulated by SFA.

2 The Government announced on 20 May 1997 that it would create a single regulator, to be the Financial Services Authority for all financial markets, merging nine regulatory bodies including the SFA. On June 1 1998, the FSA began supplying regulatory services under contract to SFA and the other two Self-Regulating Organisations (SROs). In addition, the staff of SFA, IMRO and PIA and the Banking Supervision & Surveillance Division of the Bank of England took up their posts as employees of the FSA.

3 On 30 December 1998, the SFA issued a Press Release announcing that it had issued Intervention Orders against both Griffin and GLH requiring them to cease carrying on investment business from that date. The SFA issued the Orders on the basis that both firms may not be fit and proper to carry on investment business, that they had committed acts of misconduct under SFA Rules and

that SFA intervention was desirable for the protection of investors.

4 GLH was a clearing customer of Griffin for business contracted on derivatives exchanges. Both Griffin and GLH were unable to meet a margin call arising from Mr Park's trading through GLH. The London International Financial Futures and Options Exchange (LIFFE) declared both firms to be in default with effect from 24 December 1998.

5 GLH was a London-based company whose shareholders were independent traders trading predominantly on their own account on LIFFE and Eurex.

6 Griffin in London was a branch of a Chicago-incorporated company specialising in providing clearing facilities to traders on derivatives exchanges. Griffin's London branch acted as clearing agent for the independent traders who comprised GLH.

28 October 1999

SFA Disciplines Neil Thorneywork & Hawthorne Securities Limited

SFA has today announced that it has concluded disciplinary proceedings against Mr Neil Thorneywork and Hawthorne Securities Limited with the following outcome:-

- **Neil Thorneywork has been expelled from all SFA Registers and is required to pay £29,000 towards SFA's costs;**
- **Hawthorne Securities Limited has been expelled from SFA and is required to pay a contribution towards SFA's costs of £29,000 and to pay compensation to two former clients.**

Mr Thorneywork was the senior executive officer and principal shareholder in Hawthorne Securities Limited, a mainly private client broker based in the Birmingham area.

Between 1994 and 1998, Mr Thorneywork and Hawthorne Securities Limited, in relation to 7 clients, variously:–

- acted in direct contradiction to clients' instructions by writing index options on their portfolios;
- acted in direct contradiction to clients' instructions by selling one client's stock to meet another client's margin calls in relation to options trading;
- invested clients' funds in speculative options writing strategies when their investment objectives had been made clear as being of a highly conservative nature;
- failed to explain to clients the high risks involved in the speculative investment strategies into which their portfolios had been invested;
- deliberately misled clients as to the true value of their stock and option portfolios;
- obtained blank signed letterheads of a pension fund by misleading the trustees to be able to purport to an options clearing firm that instructions to trade in options were coming directly from that pension fund. This was after the options clearing firm had removed Mr Thorneywork's and Hawthorne Securities Limited's authorisation to issue instructions to trade on behalf of any clients;
- sought to reduce the level of clients' co-operation with SFA by sending misleading letters to those clients whose accounts SFA had indicated that they wished to investigate.

SFA found that Mr Thorneywork and Hawthorne Securities Limited were in breach of the following FSA Principles and SFA Rules:–

- Principle 1: failure to observe high standards of integrity and fair dealing;
- Principle 5: failure to give customers information in a timely and comprehensible manner to enable them to make balanced and informed decisions;
- Principle 9: failure to organise and control the internal affairs of the firm;
- Principle 10: failure to deal with SFA in an open and co-operative manner;
- Rule 5–31(1): making unsuitable investment recommendations and effecting unsuitable transactions for clients.

Mr Thorneywork and Hawthorne Securities Limited had previously been subject of Intervention Orders which took effect on the 4 March 1999 as set out in SFA Press Notice SFA3-99.

Source: Financial Services Authority

The above examples show the kind of problems that firms face when a staff member decides to break the internal and or external rules and regulations pertaining to that firm's business. The reader can look at many more examples by visiting the FSA website. In some cases it is the firm that is affected to the extent of damage to its profits. In other cases like Griffin for instance, the consequences are far greater and involve more than just the firm and the individual. There are also cases where the customer is affected.

It is easy to see why the regulators need to stamp out these kind of situations if the credibility of the financial markets is to be maintained. It is also easy to see why operations staff have a duty to report anything suspicious to their managers and or compliance officers.

Chapter 7

Operations and breaches of regulation

According to the regulators: 'There is no such thing as an inadvertent breach of regulations'

That statement is in itself enough to put some operations managers into a cold sweat and yet its logic cannot be faulted. Why when regulations are, in most cases anyway, reasonably clearly set out does a firm end up in a situation where they are in breach of them? Well there are of course many reasons why this might happen including lack of awareness, inefficiency and poor management. Occasionally there might be a series of 'unfortunate coincidences' or so-called 'mitigating circumstances' that nevertheless result in or create a failure to comply with relevant regulations, but essentially the regulator is right, irrespective of the causes in today's financial markets environment it – still should not have happened!!!

To a large degree the firm will try to mitigate against this kind of scenario happening by having management and internal audit reviews, possibly external consultants examine procedures and of course rely on the compliance function overseeing the way in which the firm operates. It is strange but it always seems a source of near panic when the imminent visit of the audit team is announced. It is comparable with the traveller approaching customs with absolutely nothing to declare and yet they break out into a cold sweat.

Everyone from the manager to the most junior staff seem to be gripped by a fear that 'something' will be found that is not complying with internal and external rules or regulations or indeed both. Perhaps it is the image of audit as some kind of a law enforcer to be feared or maybe it is the realisation that a breach of the regulations can have a significant impact and is consequently not merely a routine situation. Perhaps it just irrational behaviour in what is otherwise 'normal' people, but 'standard' jokes like 'hide the books' or 'only give them name, rank and number' betray the underlying concern.

Whatever it is, the visit of audit is bound, it seems, to be viewed with dread which is a pity because audit is not only there to protect the business but help the relevant area being audited by giving an independent view of the quality and robustness of the controls and procedures. Of course audit can produce an 'embarrassing' result and naturally the impact of an audit report that raises a few important but not business stopping points can nevertheless be blown up into a major issue.

This is the fault of inadequate and unrealistic senior management, not audit. Audit have simply done their job. So too have the operations teams but they are not perfect. The point is that between them audit, by recognising and highlighting a problem, and operations by responding will have strengthened the firm controls and its compliance.

So the operations manger needs to look at audit, and for that matter compliance, as a friend and a vital help in assessing the well being of the department and the effectiveness of the processes and procedures. Other than the use of consultants, audit is about the only way to get that independent view.

Of course some breaches of rules and regulations are more serious than the odd weakness or two, client money for instance. We must also accept that the odd weakness or two must not be allowed to continue and thus become a breach of rules or regulations that are designed to prevent a more serious situation from developing. Failure to address within a reasonable timeframe a weakness in procedures, controls or processes that do or may constitute a breach of regulations is not acceptable. Sadly in many organisations the 'minor' relatively speaking incidents of weak procedures or temporary loss of effective ones are treated as a 'disaster' whilst much more fundamental problems and situations endemic of poor management and dangerous situations go unnoticed or without any action. Yes weak procedures need to be dealt with, we noted that just now, but many things can cause them, and often these are not under the operations manager's control or maybe are very temporary situations. Lack of investment in people and or systems is often a cause of weak procedures, knowledge and skill sets and therefore a risk. Ultimately that risk can manifest itself in regulatory situation.

Whether they like this or not, senior management is responsible for this kind of scenario and basic mis-management at a senior level is a far greater risk, and particularly a regulatory risk than anything else in operations. This is recognised, as we have seen earlier, in the Principles and Conduct of Business Rules of the FSA.

The operations manager must be in a position to identify the critical rules and regulations, controls and standards. The importance of these must be impressed on the supervisors and the team. In operational risk, reputational risk is a key one and nothing is going to damage reputation like a public reprimand and or fine for breach of a key regulation like client money. Of course client money is not the only 'operations'-based regulation that can cause a problem (breaches of clearing house rules springs to mind), but it is certainly the most serious.

Look at these case studies which cover disciplinary actions brought by the Securities and Futures Authority (SFA), now merged into the FSA:

30 September 1999

SFA Disciplines Trust Financial Group (Europe) Ltd

SFA has settled disciplinary proceedings against Trust Financial Group (Europe) Ltd ('Trust Financial') as follows:

- **Trust Financial is no longer trading and has undertaken to SFA that neither it nor those connected with it will seek to conduct investment business in the U.K. without the prior consent of SFA and/or the Financial Services Authority ('the FSA'). Accordingly Trust Financial has been permitted to resign from authorisation.**
- **Trust Financial has been required to pay costs of £35,200.**

Trust Financial has admitted that:

- its monitoring of trading on customer accounts was inadequate and that between October 1995 and April 1997 it failed to act with due skill, care and diligence by failing to adequately monitor trading activity on customer accounts. (This was in breach of Principle 2 of the FSA's Statements of Principle);
- it failed to ensure that it maintained adequate financial resources between January 1996 and April 1997. (This was in breach of Principle 8 of the FSA's Statements of Principle);
- its financial records were inadequate and in breach of rules relating to records and systems of internal control between January 1996 and April 1997. (This was in breach of Rules 10–10 to 10–13); and
- it failed to organise and control its internal affairs in a responsible manner, keeping proper records between October 1995 and April 1997. (This was in breach of Principle 9 of the FSA's Statements of Principle).

Case background

Trust Financial was authorised by SFA in July 1994. It acted predominantly as an intermediate clearing broker for overseas customers introduced by (predominantly German) introducing brokers. In October 1995, Trust Financial extended its business profile to provide an execution-only service to private customers.

Prior to authorisation and being permitted to undertake private customer business, SFA advised Trust Financial that as it was acting as an intermediate clearing broker:

- it must monitor trading activity on individual customer accounts in order to ensure trading was in their customer's best interests; and
- as a number of introducing brokers had discretionary authority over the customer accounts which they had introduced to Trust Financial, the level of monitoring performed by Trust Financial would need to be increased.

Trust Financial reported to SFA that it was actively monitoring trading activity on a number of occasions between June 1995 and March 1997. The firm also reported that its operations were more than adequately resourced and that it had established a very effective compliance regime.

Following receipt of a qualified audit report in April 1997, SFA visited Trust Financial and concluded that:

- the firm was not monitoring customer accounts as required and there was evidence that customers had been disadvantaged;
- the firm had been in breach of a number of record-keeping and financial rules; its records were not sufficient to disclose the firm's financial position accurately nor to demonstrate whether it had sufficient capital to comply with its financial resources requirement;
- Trust Financial had failed to reconcile certain balances, including client balances, throughout 1996; and
- it appeared that Trust Financial had been reporting incorrect balances in its financial reporting statements to SFA.

As a result, SFA intervened against Trust Financial in May 1997 and worked with the firm to ensure an orderly run down of the business. The enforcement proceedings then followed.

Note

1 SFA is the regulatory organisation established under the Financial Services Act 1986 with responsibility for regulating members of all the organised City investment markets, i.e. the stock market, eurobond, financial futures, commodity futures markets and also corporate finance specialists and off-market traders. Around 1,350 firms are regulated by the SFA.

2 The Government announced on 20 May 1997 that it would create a single regulator for all financial markets merging nine regulatory

bodies including SFA. On June 1 1998, the FSA began to supply regulatory services under contract to SFA and the other two Self-Regulating Organisations (SROs). In addition, the staff of SFA, IMRO and PIA and the Supervision & Surveillance Division of the Bank of England took up their new posts as employees of the FSA.

Regulation in fund management

Regulation in fund management is crucial to the investor. It provides the protection that matters so much. Not surprisingly the regulators have little time for breaches of regulation in this field and any firm that does fall foul of the regulator can expect to be very carefully watched in the future, assuming they have not suffered a move to restrict or shut down their business.

Not only is a breach embarrassing, it can also be financially damaging. The mis-pricing of assets can be example. The FSA has laid down 'unequivocal' guidelines for what will happen in retail funds. If the pricing of for example a unit trust's assets is incorrect by more than 0.5%, the manager will have to either compensate the client or if the client has profited, accept and make good the loss (Table 7.1).

It should be noted that this 0.5% is only for the occasional error in pricing and any manager that was consistently having problems would be dealt with.

It is also important to remember that the manager is responsible for the fund administration, be it provided internally or externally by another firm. The manager can outsource the function but not the responsibility. Operations managers in fund management companies or firms servicing them, including custodians, fund administrators, prime brokers, brokers and banks, need to understand the regulations applicable to fund management. Let us look at some of the regulations that apply.

Table 7.1

Situation	Price incorrect by less than 0.5%	Price incorrect by more than 0.5%
Dealings between Fund and Manager		
Fund Gains (creation too high or cancellation too low)	Trustee will normally take no action[1]	Trustee to compensate manager from fund
Fund Loses (creation too low or cancellation too high)	Trustee will normally take no action[1]	Trustee directs Manager to compensate fund
Dealings between Unit Holders and Manager		
Incoming Unit Holder Gains (offer price too low)	No action	Manager unlikely to seek compensation from holder
Incoming Unit Holder Loses (offer price too high)	Trustee will normally take no action	Manager to compensate incoming unit holder
Outgoing Unit Holder Gains (bid price too high)	No action	Manager unlikely to seek compensation from unit holder
Out Going Unit Holder Loses (bid price too low)	Trustee will normally take no action	Manager to compensate outgoing unit holders

[1] The trustee can decide to take action but is unlikely to do so.

For commercial considerations, the manager is unlikely, and may find it legally impossible, to pursue unit holders to reclaim any advantage created by the manager's failure to correctly price the units.

Regulation and derivatives

Derivatives have, wrongly, a negative image in many quarters which is odd for an instrument that is designed to transfer risk. High profile problems and indeed catastrophes that have affected some organisations using derivatives are often cited as reasons why derivatives should not be used.

This is wrong and indeed potentially damaging to the investor as the use of derivatives can not only reduce risk but also improve the performance of investments.

What is clear however is that there needs to be regulation over the use of derivatives just as there is for most other types of instrument, like high yield or junk bonds, used in the financial and commodity markets? When the use of, say, a futures contract is totally inappropriate for a fund or investor, then quite rightly there is regulation, either from the main regulatory body or, say, the trustees that prevent its use.

There is also regulation over the trading of the products, particularly those traded on an exchange, where the exchange sets out rules and regulations and so too does the clearing house associated with the exchange.

Dealing with these regulations will be influenced by the nature of the firm and the reasons why and how derivatives are being used. For example the firm that is a member of an exchange and the clearing house has rules and regulations it must comply with. Some of those rules will also apply directly or mostly indirectly to the clients of that firm.

For example, the minimum margin requirement levied on the clearing member must be charged to their clients. The firm is free to levy a higher rate but it cannot charge less. Then there is the requirement on some markets for the name of the party behind 'large' orders to be made available to the regulators and in some cases there are limits on the size of position that any one firm or client may hold.

Part of the problem is that the rules are not uniform and so life is difficult for the operations teams. High quality knowledge of market practices and effective controls are needed if that dreaded 'inadvertent breach' is not to occur.

Within fund management there are restrictions on the use of derivatives including limits on the percentage of a portfolio that can be held as derivatives.

Complying with industry recommendations

As we can see, the failure to meet regulatory standards is no small matter and could result in a firm being unable to undertake certain business activity. The regulatory risk element of operational risk is a major one but so too are issues surrounding the failure to comply, adopt and address key industry recommendations. From a business point of view there are serious problems if operationally, the firm fails to keep pace with developments in the industry and these include the major changes that organisations like ISSA recommend. These recommendations are likely, as we know, to either become industry best practice, benchmark standards or regulation.

So what are the key recommendations that are relevant today?

ISSA recommendations 2000 & update 2001

The ISSA Recommendations 2000 – Status Report 2001 brochure is an analysis, and the conclusions drawn from the first global status survey, including a recommended action plan, is available from the ISSA website: http://www.issanet.org/

There is a downloadable 54-page Adobe Acrobat document (400 kb) of this report under the 'publications' section of the site. This report contains an amended wording of Recommendation 7. Published in April 2002. The report outlines an idea of those made by ISSA as part of their Recommendations 2000 and includes an update on how the industry is complying with them as at December 2001. Study them carefully and then relate them to you own firm. What is the impact?

The recommendations made by ISSA relating to investor protection are important to consider, particularly as we need to look at the change after the Second Networking Managers meeting in response to the survey.

The change (see page 50 of the Status Report 2001) reads as:

Recommendation 7

Regulators in each country should review whether locally domiciled institutions have a process in place that enables them to comply with the laws and regulations of the countries where their investments are placed. In turn, foreign investors should always be treated in like fashion to the indigenous investors, especially in respect to their rights to shareholder benefits.

It should not be difficult to see how the firm that is not aware of, and complying with this and the other recommendations, is likely to encounter either commercial and or regulatory problems. Participation in the debates and compilation of these organisations is a vital matter for any major firm and receiving and commenting on them is important for all firms.

Relationships in the financial markets industry are a source of risk and regulation. 'Know Your Customer' is prevalent, as we saw in Chapter 5 in areas like money laundering, as well as in relation to client money and FSA Principles to name but a few.

Due diligence

Failure to properly assess and understand the counterparty and the relationship is a risk and so firms undertaking business with or for another party must apply suitable levels of controls before entering into any agreements or transactions, etc.

This is known as 'due diligence' and covers many areas so that an operations teams are faced with any number of situations where the firm is required to undertake due diligence in its dealings with and relationships with counterparties of varying sorts.

By way of example we can look at the situation regarding a client, say a fund manager, considering counterparties for a custody and administration service. We looked at the regulation covering custody in Chapter 3.

The extent of the enquiry and assessment that is needed can be illustrated by the following example RFP that includes formats from various sources and compiled by organisations such as the Alternative Investment Management Association (AIMA) for what should be included in an RFP.

Please note that AIMA has several suggested RFP formats and those interested can purchase copies from AIMA via their website www.aima.org

Illustration of the content of a request for proposal

A RFP will be issued to possible counterparties and will seek to provide an indication of the capabilities of the counterparty and also how the counterparty marries up to the operational, credit and risk issues and requirements of the client.

The RFP will be broken up into sections addressing different elements of the expected/required service.

The following is a *short* version of a RFP for illustrative purposes:

Company Details	
Group Overview	Structure and offices
	Turnover
	Balance Sheet

Service Details	
Number of Clients	Broken down into size and geographical location
Funds/Assets Managed	Broken down by types of client and products
Markets Covered Directly	Presence in a Group name and products covered
Markets Covered via Sub custodian	Presence via an agent and products covered
Core Services Offered	Details of all services offered
Value Added Services Offered	Details of all services offered
Operational Overview	Details of operational structure
	Management structure/ team including experience
	Staffing levels and location
	Client Services Provision
	Overview of timing/ deadlines and routings of instruction for critical processes

	Systems utilised and ability to provide technology-based services to clients
Risk Management	Overview of the risk management process
	Disaster Recovery capability
	Management of exposures
	Risk management services offered
Performance	Illustration of internal and external benchmarks
	Training and development policies for staff
	Overview of content of the Service Level Agreement (SLA)
Costs	Indication of cost basis and methods of charging
Developments	Overview of current and planned developments to the services offered

Source: thedsc.portfolio

It is clear from the by no means exhaustive illustration above that performance and innovation are critically important in a highly competitive market place. Clients are rightly concerned about the impact of poor services on their own business and as a consequence the Service Level Agreement becomes an important safeguard.

Compliance with not only the internal procedures but also with any regulation applicable is fundamentally important.

The RFP cannot be falsified as the consequences of misleading a potential client should not need emphasising, and the SLA is an agreement for which compliance is a prerequisite on both parties.

If an operations team cannot or does not deliver then the relationship will be irreparably damaged. Inevitably the reputation of the firm will also be damaged and there may also be serious regulatory issues that will arise, particularly if the client has been put at risk in some way.

Consider also the Financial Services Authority's (FSA) guidelines on the matter:

The FSA suggests the following should be assessed when considering an *eligible custodian*:

- Expertise and market reputation
- Performance of the services provided
- The protection afforded to the client's assets in the event of the Custodians bankruptcy
- What are the standard reports used, i.e.
- The capital of the custodian
- The credit rating
- The extent to which the custodian is regulated
- Other activities of the custodian and related firms

The FSA further suggests that where a firm intends to use an eligible custodian from within the same group as the firm, it must:

- Undertake a continuous assessment at least as rigorous as the assessment of an eligible custodian not in the same group
- Disclose in writing to the customer that it intends to use a custodian within the same group as the firm BEFORE holding the customer's safekeeping custody investment with the custodian

Stock lending

Here again the regulator sets out rules and guidelines that are perfectly reasonable given that stock lending is a potential way of generating additional revenue but at the same time increases risk.

Naturally any breach of the rules and guidelines will not be viewed in a good light so what kind of issues are we talking about?

Stock lending is a transaction that results in the temporary disposal of an investment subject to an obligation or right to reacquire the same or similar investments from the same counterparty.

Today it is big business with hedge funds in particular large borrowers of securities. Straight away we can see a possible situation arising whereby a conservative investment fund increases revenue by lending some of its securities. The borrower is a highly geared hedge fund with significant short positions and exposures in the securities. On the face of it this is surely not acceptable to the investors who have a low risk appetite.

On the other hand if the securities are being loaned via another party, for instance a custodian, there is a different risk profile provided that Rules designed to protect a customer are complied with.

For instance a firm should not undertake or otherwise engage in stock lending activity with or for a customer unless:

- The customer has consented
- The activity is subject to appropriate terms and conditions, including in the case of a private customer that they have given their prior written consent specifying the assets to be lent, the type and value of acceptable collateral from the borrower and the method and amount of remuneration due to the customer in respect of the lending
- Where an investment belonging to a private customer is lent, the firm ensures that;
  - Acceptable collateral is provided by the borrower in favour of that customer

- ◻ The current realisable value of the investment and the acceptable collateral is monitored daily
- ◻ Where the current realisable value of the collateral falls below the value of the investment, the firm provides acceptable collateral to make up the difference

From an operational viewpoint the key issues to avoiding a breach of regulations will surround establishing the lending is authorised and then ensuring that the loan terms and the revaluation of investment and collateral is undertaken.

Continuing the conditions under which a firm should not undertake stock lending activity unless:

- Where investments of more than one customer are registered or otherwise held together, none of the investments may be used unless:
  - ◻ All of the customers have consented
  - ◻ The firm alternatively has adequate systems and procedures in place to ensure that only investments belonging to customers who have given their consent are used
- Any cash or assets held in favour of a customer as collateral for stock lending must be held in accordance with the client money rules and custody rules

From the operational viewpoint the key issues here are the ability to record and recognise clients assets which are available for lending and those which are not, and also where lending or borrowing takes place that the assets are held in accordance with the client money and custody rules. To achieve this the custodial and stock lending activities will be segregated.

In addition the firm will need to have adequate documentation with both the customer and the borrower so Agreements become a key feature. This will also apply to the customer like for instance a fund where the trust deeds or Scheme Particulars will indicate whether the assets of the fund can be lent.

Chapter 8

The future of regulation

What next for regulation, regulators and the regulated?

The regulatory environment certainly changes. The formation of the Financial Services Authority as a single regulator for financial markets in the U.K. has been looked at in this book, but the following statement illustrates how the regulatory environment has changed in Japan partly in response to various scandals that were affecting the integrity of the Japanese financial markets and the potential damage that it was doing to the country.

STATEMENT BY THE COMMISSIONER

– On the Establishment of the Financial Services Agency –

The Financial Services Agency (FSA) was established on July 1, 2000, with the integration of the Financial Supervisory Agency and the Financial System Planning Bureau of the Ministry of Finance. On this occasion, I hereby announce the mission statement and the six basic policy principles of our new agency.

Mission

The FSA's mission is to make the financial system reliable and vigorous, and the financial markets fair and efficient. The FSA aims to contribute to the national welfare and economy by pursuing this mission. The financial system performs indispensable functions for the economy, transmitting funds and intermediating risks among economic entities and providing settlement services to them. Without a sound and efficient financial system, it is impossible to improve national welfare or develop the economy. The financial markets are at the core of the financial system. They need to be developed so that the users can benefit from their proper functioning fully and with confidence.

The FSA will perform its regulatory functions relying upon market discipline and the principle of self-responsibility. In light of the rapid development of financial technologies and the globalization of financial activities, the FSA strives to maintain high expertise and to ensure consistency between its policies and international rules and practices. In doing so, the FSA endeavors to protect depositors, policyholders, investors, and other users of the financial system, and also to make the financial markets more convenient for them. Clarity of rules is at the FSA's priority and the FSA will implement them promptly and correctly. The FSA intends to enhance the transparency of its policy planning and administrative procedures. The FSA is committed to be accountable in all stages of its activities.

The FSA is responsible for all aspects of financial regulation, from the designing of financial systems to inspection, supervision, and surveillance of financial activities. The FSA is also responsible for all kinds of financial services, such as banking, securities business, and insurance. The FSA intends to make full use of these capacities to achieve timely and consistent implementation of policies in order to respond to challenges arising from changes in the financial environment.

Basic Policies

1 Establishing a reliable and vigorous financial system

Efforts have been made to stabilize Japan's financial system. As a result, it has on the whole regained its stability. In the light of the scheduled termination on March 31, 2002 of the emergency measure to protect all bank deposits, the FSA will work further to strengthen the financial system. As the financial system constitutes a basis for all economic activities, the FSA seeks to develop a vigorous financial system and to promote competition so as to revitalize the national economy. Further, the FSA seeks to ensure the smooth flow of credit in order that sufficient capital will be supplied to small and medium sized enterprises and new industries, thus contributing to the growth of the national economy.

2 **Developing a state-of-the-art financial infrastructure**

With the development of financial technology and information and communication technology, and the globalization of financial and economic activities, cross-sectoral financial products and services are being rapidly developed. User-friendly financial markets attract international capital. Such tendencies will accelerate further. In light of these, the FSA aims to develop a user-friendly financial infrastructure, in order to sustain and improve the role of the Japanese markets in the world. The market infrastructure shall be at the state-of-the-art in the new millennium.

3 **Development and proper implementation of regulations to protect users**

With the variety of financial products and services being widely used, the FSA intends to create the framework for the protection of users of financial products and services so that they can conduct financial transactions with confidence under the principle of self-responsibility. For that purpose, the FSA will develop and implement regulations to protect users and will expand its consumer education efforts so as to promote public understanding in financial products and financial transactions.

4 **Ensuring transparency and fairness in financial administration based on clear rules (market discipline and the principle of self-responsibility)**

The FSA is committed to achieving transparent and fair financial administration in every respect under clear rules based on market discipline and the principle of self-responsibility. Accordingly, in the areas of inspection, supervision, and surveillance, the FSA intends to ensure the efficiency and effectiveness of its activities and clarity of its rules, improve administrative procedures, and strengthen public relations. The FSA will promote enhanced disclosure by financial institutions to further improve transparency of their business, to place market discipline on them, and to establish the principle of self-responsibility among depositors, etc.

5 Enhancing the expertise and foresight of the staff and improving the administrative structure

The FSA seeks to enhance the expertise and foresight of its staff to respond adequately and rapidly to changes in the financial environment such as the growing complexity of financial activities and the development of information and communication technology. From this viewpoint, the FSA seeks to train and secure staff with expertise and broad perspectives by improving personnel training, envisaging the establishment of an institute for financial studies, and developing a strong organizational structure.

6 Reinforcing cooperation with foreign regulators and contributing to international rule setting

The FSA will strengthen cooperation with foreign financial regulatory authorities and promote exchange of information to respond to the globalization of financial activities and transactions. The FSA intends to expand communication with the international community. The FSA will take the initiative in international rule-setting and in other efforts to build a resilient international financial architecture.

July 3, 2000
Financial Services Agency
The Government of Japan

Regulation changes in response to developments in the global and domestic financial markets as well as the attitudes of governments and of course the performance of the regulatory body. We saw an example of the latter with the changes made to bank surveillance in the U.K. post the collapse of Barings. So it is very much a case of what is likely to change in the markets, global economies, how well the regulator controls the risk in the markets and inevitably what the next big "disaster" is, where it occurs and how much damage is done.

The ability of the regulators to perform their function does, as was noted right at the beginning of this book, rely on the ability of firms and organisations to manage themselves effectively. That said there are developments that are undoubtedly helping the regulator to be effective. Events at WorldCom, Enron, etc. have certainly prompted questions about the role of regulators and others like auditors, but they have also been so high profile that it is very much the dubious management of the organisations concerned that have been the main focus. Demands for jail sentences and legal action were so powerful that the President himself became involved in demanding tough action against the managers responsible and issued a stark warning to companies to clean up their act and to stop damaging the U.S.

We have also had the "Spritzer" settlement in relation to the scandals surrounding analysts that has cost the major financial firms $millions and the ongoing and steadily increasing backlash against the general corporate rip-offs like "golden hellos and goodbyes". This is when so-called top people have come in and simply devalued share prices and often damaged companies and yet walk away with massive pay offs. This cosy "club" is now the subject of regulatory and shareholder scrutiny and those benefiting from "sleaze and greed" are now publicly shamed.

The power of the regulator is significant and yet while it is the "deterrent" effect that is often the most powerful weapon, once a problem occurs it can still "help" the regulator.

You can bet that just like after Barings, there were many senior managers and directors in many different organisations running round like headless chickens in case something was "wrong" in their businesses.

So the regulator was to some extent helped by the problem and for a while at least it is reasonable to assume that regulatory issues and compliance are high on the agenda at senior management level. This in turn will lead to higher levels of compliance within organisations in the markets, not least because any organisation knows that in the current climate if it is discovered to be in serious breach of regulations then the retribution will be very, very severe.

Also helping the regulators is the issue of operational risk and in particular "reputation risk". It is, in an increasingly competitive environment, disastrous for any firm to be publicly reprimanded by a regulator and particularly where any client money rules or misuse of client assets is involved.

Choice of counterparty for many institutions traditionally revolved around trading costs and capital/rating issues. Today these are still important but so too is reputation. Many trustees and risk managers will want details of any regulatory reprimands before sanctioning a relationship and may require a presentation on risk and regulation awareness by the potential counterparty. As a result the more enlightened firms will make sure that training and competence requirements are met, but also that internal awareness of regulatory and reputation risk is provided at every level.

Automation is also making the regulators gathering of critical data easier and much quicker. In Chapter 3 we commented on how electronic trading systems were able to send trade data to the regulator in a very short timeframe from the actual time of the trade but the enhancement of systems in firms is also providing internally much better control and thereby reducing, in theory anyway, the risk of a breach of regulations.

Harmonisation of regulation is often talked about and clearly there is progress towards this as we have seen in Europe, and yet the regulators will never be able to completely eradicate malpractice, fraud and criminal activity. Like it or not cash is king and the temptation to become wealthy will always be too much for some people.

Operational functions are part of the overall battle to prevent crime in the financial markets but they are only a part. Regulation, as an operations issue, is nevertheless growing in importance.

Recognition of operations regulatory importance can be seen in the competency standards regulatory bodies are introducing. As a profession the operations function needs high quality people with knowledge, experience and the ability to manage risk as well as processes.

The future of regulation will lie in defeating the corporate sleaze, the criminal activity in the financial markets and the huge and ever changing systemic risk to the financial markets.

It will achieve this through greater awareness and enforcing of its powers and also by increasing the standards, performance and ethicality of the markets and their participants.

The operations function will be part of this and so the future of regulation and the operations function is intrinsically linked.

Appendix A

The principles

1. **Integrity**
   A *firm* must conduct its business with integrity
2. **Skills, care and diligence**
   A *firm* must conduct its business with due skill, care and diligence
3. **Management and control**
   A *firm* must take reasonable care to organise and control its affairs responsibly and effectively, with adequate risk management systems
4. **Financial prudence**
   A *firm* must maintain adequate financial resources
5. **Market conduct**
   A *firm* must observe proper standards of market conduct
6. **Customers' interests**
   A *firm* must pay due regard to the interest of its *customers* and treat them fairly
7. **Communications with clients**
   A *firm* must pay due regard to the information needs of its *clients*, and communicate information to them in a way which is clear, fair and not misleading
8. **Conflict of interest**
   A *firm* must manage conflicts of interest fairly, both between itself and its *customers* and between a *customer* and another *client*
9. **Customers: relationships of trust**
   A *firm* must take reasonable care to ensure the suitability of its advice and discretionary decisions for any *customer* who is entitled to rely upon its judgement
10. **Clients' assets**
    A *firm* must arrange adequate protection for *clients*' assets when it is responsible for them
11. **Relations with regulators**
    A *firm* must deal with its regulators in an open and cooperative way, and must disclose to the *FSA* appropriately anything relating to the *firm* of which the *FSA* would reasonably expect notice

Source: FSA handbook Release 001
December 2001

Appendix B

Global master securities lending agreement

AGREEMENT

BETWEEN:

("**Party A**") a company incorporated under the laws of
of acting through a Designated Office; and

("**Party B**") a company incorporated under the laws of
of acting through a Designated Office.

1. **APPLICABILITY**

1.1 From time to time the parties may enter into transactions in which one party ("**Lender**") will transfer to the other ("**Borrower**") securities and financial instruments ("**Securities**") against the transfer of Collateral (as defined in paragraph 2) with a simultaneous agreement by Borrower to transfer to Lender Securities equivalent to such Securities on a fixed date or on demand against the transfer to Borrower by Lender of assets equivalent to such Collateral.

1.2 Each such transaction shall be referred to in this Agreement as a "**Loan**" and shall be governed by the terms of this Agreement, including the supplemental terms and conditions contained in the Schedule and any Addenda or Annexures attached hereto, unless otherwise agreed in writing.

1.3 Either party may perform its obligations under this Agreement either directly or through a Nominee.

The London Stock Exchange website www.londonstockexchange.com

2. **INTERPRETATION**

2.1 In this Agreement:–

"**Act of Insolvency**" means in relation to either Party

(i) its making a general assignment for the benefit of, or entering into a reorganisation, arrangement, or composition with creditors; or

(ii) its stating in writing that it is unable to pay its debts as they become due; or

(iii) its seeking, consenting to or acquiescing in the appointment of any trustee, administrator, receiver or liquidator or analogous officer of it or any material part of its property; or

(iv) the presentation or filing of a petition in respect of it (other than by the other Party to this Agreement in respect of any obligation under this Agreement) in any court or before any agency alleging or for the bankruptcy, winding-up or insolvency of such Party (or any analogous proceeding) or seeking any reorganisation, arrangement, composition, re-adjustment, administration, liquidation, dissolution or similar relief under any present or future statute, law or regulation, such petition not having been stayed or dismissed within 30 days of its filing (except in the case of a petition for winding-up or any analogous proceeding in respect of which no such 30 day period shall apply); or

(v) the appointment of a receiver, administrator, liquidator or trustee or analogous officer of such Party over all or any material part of such Party's property; or

(vi) the convening of any meeting of its creditors for the purpose of considering a voluntary arrangement as referred to in Section 3 of the Insolvency Act 1986 (or any analogous proceeding);

"**Alternative Collateral**" means Collateral having a Market Value equal to the Collateral delivered pursuant to paragraph 5 and provided by way of substitution in accordance with the provisions of paragraph 5.3;

"**Base Currency**" means the currency indicated in paragraph 2 of the Schedule;

"**Business Day**" means a day other than a Saturday or a Sunday on which banks and securities markets are open for business generally in each place stated in paragraph 3 of the Schedule and, in relation to the delivery or redelivery of any of the following in relation to any Loan, in the place(s) where the relevant Securities, Equivalent Securities, Collateral or Equivalent Collateral are to be delivered;

"**Cash Collateral**" means Collateral that takes the form of a transfer of currency;

"**Close of Business**" means the time at which the relevant banks, securities exchanges or depositaries close in the business centre in which payment is to be made or Securities or Collateral is to be delivered;

"**Collateral**" means such securities or financial instruments or transfers of currency as are referred to in the table set out under paragraph I of the Schedule as being acceptable or any combination thereof as agreed between the Parties in relation to any particular Loan and which are delivered by Borrower to Lender in accordance with this Agreement and shall include Alternative Collateral;

"**Defaulting Party**" shall have the meaning given in paragraph 14;

"**Designated Office**" means the branch or office of a Party which is specified as such in paragraph 4 of the Schedule or such other branch or office as may be agreed to in writing by the Parties;

"**Equivalent**" or "**equivalent to**" in relation to any Securities or Collateral provided under this Agreement means securities, together with cash or other property (in the case of Collateral) as the case may be, of an identical type, nominal value, description and amount to particular Securities or Collateral, as the case may be, so provided. If and to the extent that such Securities or Collateral, as the case may be, consists of securities that are partly paid or have been converted, subdivided, consolidated, made the subject of a takeover, rights of pre-emption, rights to receive securities or a certificate which may at a future date be exchanged for securities, the expression shall include such securities or other assets to which Lender or Borrower as the case may be, is entitled following the occurrence of the relevant event, and, if appropriate, the giving of the relevant notice in accordance with paragraph 6.4 and provided that Lender or Borrower, as the case may be, has paid to the other Party all and any sums due in respect thereof. In the event that such Securities or Collateral, as the case may be, have been redeemed, are partly paid, are the subject of a capitalisation issue or are subject to an event similar to any of the foregoing events described in this paragraph, the expression shall have the following meanings:

(a) in the case of redemption, a sum of money equivalent to the proceeds of the redemption;

(b) in the case of a call on partly paid securities, securities equivalent to the relevant Loaned Securities or Collateral, as the case may be, provided that Lender shall have paid Borrower, in respect of Loaned Securities, and Borrower shall have paid to Lender, in respect of Collateral, an amount of money equal to the sum due in respect of the call;

(c) in the case of a capitalisation issue, securities equivalent to the relevant Loaned Securities or Collateral, as the case may be, together with the securities allotted by way of bonus thereon;

(d) in the case of any event similar to any of the foregoing events described in this paragraph, securities equivalent to the Loaned Securities or the relevant Collateral, as the case may be, together with or replaced by a sum of money or securities or other property equivalent to that received in respect of such Loaned Securities or Collateral, as the case may be, resulting from such event;

"**Income**" means any interest, dividends or other distributions of any kind whatsoever with respect to any Securities or Collateral;

"**Income Payment Date**", with respect to any Securities or Collateral means the date on which Income is paid in respect of such Securities or Collateral, or, in the case of registered Securities or Collateral, the date by reference to which particular registered holders are identified as being entitled to payment of Income;

"**Letter of Credit**" means an irrevocable, non-negotiable letter of credit in a form, and from a bank, acceptable to Lender;

"**Loaned Securities**" means Securities which are the subject of an outstanding Loan;

"**Margin**" shall have the meaning specified in paragraph I of the Schedule with reference to the table set out therein;

"**Market Value**" means:

(a) in relation to the valuation of Securities, Equivalent Securities, Collateral or Equivalent Collateral (other than Cash Collateral or a Letter of Credit):

(i) such price as is equal to the market quotation for the bid price of such Securities, Equivalent Securities, Collateral and/or Equivalent Collateral as derived from a reputable pricing information service reasonably chosen in good faith by Lender; or

(ii) if unavailable the market value thereof as derived from the prices or rates bid by a reputable dealer for the relevant instrument reasonably chosen in good faith by Lender,

in each case at Close of Business on the previous Business Day or, at the option of either Party where in its reasonable opinion there has been an exceptional movement in the price of the asset in question since such time, the latest available price; plus (in each case)

(iii) the aggregate amount of Income which has accrued but not yet been paid in respect of the Securities, Equivalent Securities, Collateral or Equivalent Collateral concerned to the extent not included in such price,

(provided that the price of Securities, Equivalent Securities, Collateral or Equivalent Collateral that are suspended shall (for the purposes of paragraph 5) be nil unless the Parties otherwise agree and (for all other purposes) shall be the price of such Securities, Equivalent Securities, Collateral or Equivalent Collateral, as the case may be, as of Close of Business on the dealing day in the relevant market last preceding the date of suspension or a commercially reasonable price agreed between the Parties;

(b) in relation to a Letter of Credit the face or stated amount of such Letter of Credit; and

(c) in relation to Cash Collateral the amount of the currency concerned;

"**Nominee**" means an agent or a nominee appointed by either Party to accept delivery of; hold or deliver Securities, Equivalent Securities, Collateral and/or Equivalent Collateral or to receive or make payments on its behalf;

"**Non-Defaulting Party**" shall have the meaning given in paragraph 14;

"**Parties**" means Lender and Borrower and "Party" shall be construed accordingly;

"**Posted Collateral**" has the meaning given in paragraph 5.4;

"**Required Collateral Value**" shall have the meaning given in paragraph 5.4;

"**Settlement Date**" means the date upon which Securities are transferred to Borrower in accordance with this Agreement.

2.2 Headings

All headings appear for convenience only and shall not affect the interpretation of this Agreement.

2.3 Market terminology

Notwithstanding the use of expressions such as "borrow", "lend", "Collateral", "Margin" "redeliver" etc. which are used to reflect terminology used in the market for transactions of the kind provided for in this Agreement, title to Securities "borrowed" or "lent" and "Collateral" provided in accordance with this Agreement shall pass from one Party to another as provided for in this Agreement, the Party obtaining such title being obliged to redeliver Equivalent Securities or Equivalent Collateral as the case may be.

2.4 **Currency conversions**

For the purposes of determining any prices, sums or values (including Market Value, Required Collateral Value, Relevant Value, Bid Value and Offer Value for the purposes of paragraphs 5 and 10 of this Agreement) prices, sums or values stated in currencies other than the Base Currency shall be converted into the Base Currency at the latest available spot rate of exchange quoted by a bank selected by Lender (or if an Event of Default has occurred in relation to Lender, by Borrower) in the London interbank market for the purchase of the Base Currency with the currency concerned on the day on which the calculation is to be made or, if that day is not a Business Day the spot rate of exchange quoted at Close of Business on the immediately preceding Business Day.

2.5 The parties confirm that introduction of and/or substitution (in place of an existing currency) of a new currency as the lawful currency of a country shall not have the effect of altering, or discharging, or excusing performance under, any term of the Agreement or any Loan thereunder, nor give a party the right unilaterally to alter or terminate the Agreement or any Loan thereunder. Securities will for the purposes of this Agreement be regarded as equivalent to other securities notwithstanding that as a result of such introduction and/or substitution those securities have been redenominated into the new currency or the nominal value of the securities has changed in connection with such redenomination.

2.6 **Modifications etc. to legislation**

Any reference in this Agreement to an act, regulation or other legislation shall include a reference to any statutory modification or re-enactment thereof for the time being in force.

3. LOANS OF SECURITIES

Lender will lend Securities to Borrower, and Borrower will borrow Securities from Lender in accordance with the terms and conditions of this Agreement. The terms of each Loan shall be agreed prior to the commencement of the relevant Loan either orally or in writing (including any agreed form of electronic communication) and confirmed in such form and on such basis as shall be agreed between the Parties. Any confirmation produced by a Party shall not supersede or prevail over the prior oral, written or electronic communication (as the case may be).

4. DELIVERY

4.1 Delivery of Securities on commencement of Loan

Lender shall procure the delivery of Securities to Borrower or deliver such Securities in accordance with this Agreement and the terms of the relevant Loan. Such Securities shall be deemed to have been delivered by Lender to Borrower on delivery to Borrower or as it shall direct of the relevant instruments of transfer, or in the case of Securities held by an agent or within a clearing or settlement system on the effective instruuctions to such agent or the operator of such system which result in such Securities being held by the operator of the clearing system for the account of the Borrower or as it shall direct, or by such other means as may be agreed.

4.2 Requirements to effect delivery

The Parties shall execute and deliver all necessary documents and give all necessary instructions to procure that all right, title and interest in:

(a) any Securities borrowed pursuant to paragraph 3;

(b) any Equivalent Securities redelivered pursuant to paragraph 8;

(c) any Collateral delivered pursuant to paragraph 5;

(d) any Equivalent Collateral redelivered pursuant to paragraphs 5 or 8;

shall pass from one Party to the other subject to the terms and conditions set out in this Agreement, on delivery or redelivery of the same in accordance with this Agreement with full title guarantee, free from all liens, charges and encumbrances. In the case of Securities, Collateral, Equivalent Securities or Equivalent Collateral title to which is registered in a computer-based system which provides for the recording and transfer of title to the same by way of book entries, delivery and transfer of title shall take place in accordance with the rules and procedures of such system as in force from time to time. The Party acquiring such right, title and interest shall have no obligation to return or redeliver any of the assets so acquired but, in so far as any Securities are borrowed or any Collateral is delivered to such Party, such Party shall be obliged, subject to the terms of this Agreement, to redeliver Equivalent Securities or Equivalent Collateral as appropriate.

4.3 Deliveries to be simultaneous unless otherwise agreed

Where under the terms of this Agreement a Party is not obliged to make a delivery unless simultaneously a delivery is made to it, subject to and without prejudice to its rights under paragraph 8.6 such Party may from time to time in accordance with market practice and in recognition of the practical difficulties in arranging simultaneous delivery of Securities,

Collateral and cash transfers waive its right under this Agreement in respect of simultaneous delivery and/or payment provided that no such waiver (whether by course of conduct or otherwise) in respect of one transaction shall bind it in respect of any other transaction.

4.4 Deliveries of Income

In respect of Income being paid in relation to any Loaned Securities or Collateral, Borrower in the case of Income being paid in respect of Loaned Securities and Lender in the case of Income being paid in respect of Collateral shall provide to the other Party, as the case may be, any endorsements or assignments as shall be customary and appropriate to effect the delivery of money or property equivalent to the type and amount of such Income to Lender, irrespective of whether Borrower received the same in respect of any Loaned Securities or to Borrower, irrespective of whether Lender received the same in respect of any Collateral.

5. COLLATERAL

5.1 Delivery of Collateral on commencement of Loan

Subject to the other provisions of this paragraph 5, Borrower undertakes to deliver to or deposit with Lender (or in accordance with Lender's instructions) Collateral simultaneously with delivery of the Securities to which the Loan relates and in any event no later than Close of Business on the Settlement Date. In respect of Collateral comprising securities, such Collateral shall be deemed to have been delivered by Borrower to Lender on delivery to Lender or as it shall direct of the relevant instruments of transfer, or in the case of such securities being held by an agent or within a clearing or settlement system, on the effective instructions to such agent or the operator of such system, which result in such securities being held by the operator of the clearing system for the account of the Lender or as it shall direct, or by such other means as may be agreed.

5.2 Deliveries through payment systems generating automatic payments

Unless otherwise agreed between the Parties, where any Securities, Equivalent Securities, Collateral or Equivalent Collateral (in the form of securities) are transferred through a book entry transfer or settlement system which automatically generates a payment or delivery, or obligation to pay or deliver, against the transfer of such securities, then:

(i) such automatically generated payment, delivery or obligation shall be treated as a payment or delivery by the transferee to the transferor, and except to the extent that it is applied to discharge an obligation of the transferee to effect payment or delivery, such payment or delivery, or obligation to pay or deliver, shall be deemed to be a transfer of Collateral or redelivery of Equivalent Collateral, as the case may be, made by the transferee until such time as the Collateral or Equivalent Collateral is substituted with other Collateral or Equivalent Collateral if an obligation to deliver other Collateral or redeliver Equivalent Collateral existed immediately prior to the transfer of Securities, Equivalent Securities, Collateral or Equivalent Collateral; and

(ii) the party receiving such substituted Collateral or Equivalent Collateral, or if no obligation to deliver other Collateral or redeliver Equivalent Collateral existed immediately prior to the transfer of Securities, Equivalent Securities, Collateral or Equivalent Collateral, the party receiving the deemed transfer of Collateral or redelivery of Equivalent Collateral, as the case may be, shall cause to be made to the other party for value the same day either, where such transfer is a payment, an irrevocable payment in the amount of such transfer or, where such transfer is a delivery, an irrevocable delivery of securities (or other property, as the case may be) equivalent to such property.

5.3 **Substitutions of Collateral**

Borrower may from time to time call for the repayment of Cash Collateral or the redelivery of Collateral equivalent to any Collateral delivered to Lender prior to the date on which the same would otherwise have been repayable or redeliverable provided that at the time of such repayment or redelivery Borrower shall have delivered or delivers Alternative Collateral acceptable to Lender and Borrower is in compliance with paragraph 5.4 or paragraph 5.5, as applicable.

5.4 **Marking to Market of Collateral during the currency of a Loan on aggregated basis**

Unless paragraph 1.3 of the Schedule indicates that paragraph 5.5 shall apply in lieu of this paragraph 5.4, or unless otherwise agreed between the Parties:

(i) the aggregate Market Value of the Collateral delivered to or deposited with Lender (excluding any Equivalent Collateral repaid or redelivered under Paragraphs 5.4(ii) or 5.5(ii) (as the case may be) ("**Posted Collateral**") in respect of all Loans outstanding under this Agreement shall equal the aggregate of the Market Value of the Loaned Securities and the applicable Margin (the "**Required Collateral Value**") in respect of such Loans;

(ii) if at any time on any Business Day the aggregate Market Value of the Posted Collateral in respect of all Loans outstanding under this Agreement exceeds the aggregate of the Required Collateral Values in respect of such Loans, Lender shall (on demand) repay and/or redeliver, as the case may be, to Borrower such Equivalent Collateral as will eliminate the excess;

(iii) if at any time on any Business Day the aggregate Market Value of the Posted Collateral in respect of all Loans outstanding under this Agreement falls below the aggregate of Required Collateral Values in respect of all such Loans, Borrower shall (on demand) provide such further Collateral to Lender as will eliminate the deficiency.

5.5 **Marking to Market of Collateral during the currency of a Loan on a Loan by Loan basis**

If paragraph 1.3 of the Schedule indicates this paragraph 5.5 shall apply in lieu of paragraph 5.4, the Posted Collateral in respect of any Loan shall bear from day to day and at any time the same proportion to the Market Value of the Loaned Securities as the Posted Collateral bore at the commencement of such Loan. Accordingly:

(i) the Market Value of the Posted Collateral to be delivered or deposited while the Loan continues shall be equal to the Required Collateral Value;

(ii) if at any time on any Business Day the Market Value of the Posted Collateral in respect of any Loan exceeds the Required Collateral Value in respect of such Loan, Lender shall (on demand) repay and/or redeliver, as the case may be, to Borrower such Equivalent Collateral as will eliminate the excess; and

(iii) if at any time on any Business Day the Market Value of the Posted Collateral falls below the Required Collateral Value, Borrower shall (on demand) provide such further Collateral to Lender as will eliminate the deficiency.

5.6 **Requirements to redeliver excess Collateral**

Where paragraph 5.4 applies, unless paragraph 1.4 of the Schedule indicates that this paragraph 5.6 does not apply, if a Party (the "**first Party**") would, but for this paragraph 5.6, be required under paragraph 5.4 to provide further Collateral or redeliver Equivalent Collateral in circumstances where the other Party (the "**second Party**") would, but for this paragraph 5.6, also be required to or provide Collateral or redeliver Equivalent Collateral under paragraph 5.4, then the Market Value of the Collateral or Equivalent Collateral deliverable by the first Party ("**X**") shall be set-off against the Market Value of the Collateral or Equivalent Collateral deliverable by the second Party ("**Y**") and the only obligation of the Parties under paragraph 5.4 shall be, where X exceeds Y, an obligation of the first Party, or where Y exceeds X, an obligation of the second Party to repay and/or (as the case may be) redeliver Equivalent Collateral or to deliver further Collateral having a Market Value equal to the difference between X and Y.

5.7 Where Equivalent Collateral is repaid or redelivered (as the case may be) or further Collateral is provided by a Party under paragraph 5.6, the Parties shall agree to which Loan or Loans such repayment, redelivery or further provision is to be attributed and failing agreement it shall be attributed, as determined by the Party making such repayment, redelivery or further provision to the earliest outstanding Loan and, in the case of a repayment or redelivery up to the point at which the Market Value of Collateral in respect of such Loan equals the Required Collateral Value in respect of such Loan, and then to the next earliest outstanding Loan up to the similar point and so on.

5.8 **Timing of repayments of excess Collateral or deliveries of further Collateral**

Where any Equivalent Collateral fails to be repaid or redelivered (as the case may be) or further Collateral is to be provided under this paragraph 5, unless otherwise agreed between the Parties, it shall be delivered on the same Business Day as the relevant demand. Equivalent Collateral comprising securities shall be deemed to have been delivered by Lender to Borrower on delivery to Borrower or as it shall direct of the relevant instruments of transfer, or in the case of such securities being held by an agent or within a clearing or settlement system on the effective instructions to such agent or the operator of such system which result in such securities being held by the operator of the clearing system for the account of the Borrower or as it shall direct or by such other means as may be agreed.

5.9 **Substitutions and extensions of Letters of Credit**

Where Collateral is a Letter of Credit, Lender may by notice to Borrower require that Borrower, on the Business Day following the date of delivery of such notice, substitute Collateral consisting of cash or other Collateral acceptable to Lender for the Letter of Credit. Prior to the expiration of any Letter of Credit supporting Borrower's obligations hereunder, Borrower shall, no later than 10.30a.m. U.K. time on the second Business Day prior to the date such Letter of Credit expires, obtain an extension of the expiration of such Letter of Credit or replace such Letter of Credit by providing Lender with a substitute Letter of Credit in an amount at least equal to the amount of the Letter of Credit tor which it is substituted.

6. DISTRIBUTIONS AND CORPORATE ACTIONS

6.1 Manufactured Payments

Where Income is paid in relation to any Loaned Securities or Collateral (other than Cash Collateral) on or by reference to an Income Payment Date Borrower, in the case of Loaned Securities, and Lender, in the case of Collateral, shall, on the date of the payment of such Income, or on such other date as the Parties may from time to time agree, (the "**Relevant Payment Date**") pay and deliver a sum of money or property equivalent to the type and amount of such Income that, in the case of Loaned Securities, Lender would have been entitled to receive had such Securities not been loaned to Borrower and had been retained by Lender on the Income Payment Date, and, in the case of Collateral, Borrower would have been entitled to receive had such Collateral not been provided to Lender and had been retained by Borrower on the Income Payment Date unless a different sum is agreed between the Parties.

6.2 **Income in the form of Securities**

Where Income, in the form of securities, is paid in relation to any Loaned Securities or Collateral, such securities shall be added to such Loaned Securities or Collateral (and shall constitute Loaned Securities or Collateral, as the case may be, and be part of the relevant Loan) and will not be delivered to Lender, in the case of Loaned Securities, or to Borrower, in the case of Collateral, until the end of the relevant Loan, provided that the Lender or Borrower (as the case may be) fulfils their obligations under paragraph 5.4 or 5.5 (as applicable) with respect to the additional Loaned Securities or Collateral, as the case may be.

6.3 **Exercise of voting rights**

Where any voting rights fail to be exercised in relation to any Loaned Securities or Collateral, neither Borrower, in the case of Equivalent Securities, nor Lender in the case of Equivalent Collateral, shall have any obligation to arrange for voting rights of that kind to be exercised in accordance with the instructions of the other Party in relation to the Securities borrowed by it or transferred to it by way of Collateral, as the case may be, unless otherwise agreed between the Parties.

6.4 **Corporate actions**

Where, in respect of any Loaned Securities or any Collateral, any rights relating to conversion, sub-division, consolidation, pre-emption, rights arising under a takeover offer, rights to receive securities or a certificate which may at a future date be exchanged for securities or other rights, including those requiring election by the holder for the time being of such Securities or Collateral, become exercisable prior to the redelivery of Equivalent Securities or Equivalent Collateral, then Lender or Borrower, as the case may be, may, within a reasonable time before the latest time for the exercise of the right or option give written notice to the other Party that on redelivery of Equivalent Securities or Equivalent Collateral, as the case may be, it wishes to receive Equivalent Securities or Equivalent Collateral in such form as will arise if the right is exercised or, in the case of a right which may be exercised in more than one manner, is exercised as is specified in such written notice.

7. RATES APPLICABLE TO LOANED SECURITIES AND CASH COLLATERAL

7.1 Rates in respect of Loaned Securities

In respect of each Loan, Borrower shall pay to Lender, in the manner prescribed in subparagraph 7.3, sums calculated by applying such rate as shall be agreed between the Parties from time to time to the daily Market Value of the Loaned Securities.

7.2 Rates in respect of Cash Collateral

Where Cash Collateral is deposited with Lender in respect of any Loan, Lender shall pay to Borrower, in the manner prescribed in paragraph 7.3, sums calculated by applying such rates as shall be agreed between the Parties from time to time to the amount of such Cash Collateral. Any such payment due to Borrower may be set-off against any payment due to Lender pursuant to paragraph 7.1.

7.3 Payment of rates

In respect of each Loan, the payments referred to in paragraph 7.1 and 7.2 shall accrue daily in respect of the period commencing on and inclusive of the Settlement Date and terminating on and exclusive of the Business Day upon which Equivalent Securities are redelivered or Cash Collateral is repaid. Unless otherwise agreed, the sums so accruing in respect of each calendar month shall be paid in arrear by the relevant Party not later than the Business Day which is one week after the last Business Day of the calendar month to which such payments relate or such other date as the Parties shall from time to time agree.

8. REDELIVERY OF EQUIVALENT SECURITIES

8.1 Delivery of Equivalent Securities on termination of a Loan

Borrower shall procure the redelivery of Equivalent Securities to Lender or redeliver Equivalent Securities in accordance with this Agreement and the terms of the relevant Loan on termination of the Loan. Such Equivalent Securities shall be deemed to have been delivered by Borrower to Lender on delivery to Lender or as it shall direct of the relevant instruments of transfer, or in the case of Equivalent Securities held by an agent or within a clearing or settlement system on the effective instructions to such agent or the operator of such system which result in such Equivalent Securities being held by the operator of the clearing system for the account of the Lender or as it shall direct, or by such other means as may be agreed. For the avoidance of doubt any reference in this Agreement or in any other agreement or communication between the Parties (howsoever expressed) to an obligation to redeliver or account for or act in relation to Loaned Securities shall accordingly be construed as a reference to an obligation to redeliver or account for or act in relation to Equivalent Securities.

8.2 **Lender's right to terminate a Loan**

Subject to paragraph 10 and the terms of the relevant Loan. Lender shall be entitled to terminate a Loan and to call for the redelivery of all or any Equivalent Securities at any time by giving notice on any Business Day of not less than the standard settlement time for such Equivalent Securities on the exchange or in the clearing organisation through which the Loaned Securities were originally delivered. Borrower shall redeliver such Equivalent Securities not later than the expiry of such notice in accordance with Lender's instructions.

8.3 **Borrower's right to terminate a Loan**

Subject to the terms of the relevant Loan, Borrower shall be entitled at any time to terminate a Loan and to redeliver all and any Equivalent Securities due and outstanding to Lender in accordance with Lender's instructions and Lender shall accept such redelivery

8.4 **Redelivery of Equivalent Collateral on termination of a Loan**

On the date and time that Equivalent Securities are required to be redelivered by Borrower on the termination of a Loan, Lender shall simultaneously (subject to paragraph 5.4 if applicable) repay to Borrower any Cash Collateral or, as the case may be, redeliver Collateral equivalent to the Collateral provided by Borrower pursuant to paragraph 5 in respect of such Loan. For the avoidance of doubt any reference in this Agreement or in any other agreement or communication between the Parties (however expressed) to an obligation to redeliver or aecount for or act in relation to Collateral shall accordingly be construed as a reference to an obligation to redeliver or account for or act in relation to Equivalent Collateral

8.5 **Redelivery of Letters of Credit**

Where a Letter of Credit is provided by way of Collateral, the obligation to redeliver Equivalent Collateral is satisfied by Lender redelivering for cancellation thc Letter of Credit so provided. or where the Letter of Credit is provided in respect of more than one Loan, by Lender consenting to a reduction in the value of the Letter of Credit

8.6 **Redelivery obligations to be reciprocal**

Neither Party shall be obliged to make delivery (or make a payment as the case may be, to the other unless it is satisfied that the other Party will make such delivery (or make an appropriate payment as the case may be) to it. If it is not so satisfied (whether because an Event of Default has occurred in respect of the other Party or otherwise) it shall notify the other party and unless that other Party has made arrangements which are sufficient to assure full delivery (or the appropriate payment as the case may be) to the notifying Party, the notifying Party shall (provided it is itself in a position, and willing, to perform its own obligations) be entitled to withhold delivery (or payment, as the case may be) to the other Party.

9 FAILURE TO REDELIVER

9.1 Borrower's failure to redeliver Equivalent Securities

(i) If Borrower does not redeliver Equivalent Securities in accordance with paragraph 8.1 or 8.2, Lender may elect to continue the Loan (which Loan, for the avoidance of doubt, shall continue to be taken into account for the purposes of paragraph 5.4 or 5.5 as applicable) provided that if Lender does not elect to continue the Loan, Lender may either by written notice to Borrower terminate the Loan forthwith and the Parties' delivery and payment obligations in respect thereof (in which case sub-paragraph (iii) below shall apply) or serve a notice of an Event of Default in accordance with paragraph 14.

(ii) Upon service of a notice to terminate the relevant Loan pursuant to paragraph 9.1(i):

(a) there shall be set-off against the Market Value of the Equivalent Securities concerned such amount of Posted Collateral chosen by Lender (calculated at its Market Value) as is equal thereto;

(b) the Parties delivery and payment obligations in relation to such assets which are set-off shall terminate;

(c) in the event that the Market Value of the Posted Collateral set-off is less than the Market Value of the Equivalent Securities concerned Borrower shall account to Lender for the shortfall; and

(d) Borrower shall account to Lender for the total costs and expenses incurred by Lender as a result thereof as set out in paragraphs 9.3 and 9.4 from the time the notice is effective.

9.2 Lender's failure to Redeliver Equivalent Collateral

(i) If Lender does not redeliver Equivalent Collateral in accordance with paragraph 8.4 or 8.5, Borrower may either by written notice to Lender terminate the Loan forthwith and the Parties' delivery and payment obligations in respect thereof (in which case sub-paragraph (ii) below shall apply) or serve a notice of an Event of Default in accordance with paragraph 14.

(ii) Upon service of a notice to terminate the relevant Loan pursuant to paragraph 9.2(i):

(a) there shall be set-off against the Market Value of the Equivalent Collateral concerned the Market Value of the Loaned Securities;

(b) the Parties delivery and payment obligations in relation to such assets which are set-off shall terminate;

(c) in the event that the Market Value of the Loaned Securities held by Borrower is less than the Market Value of the Equivalent Collateral concerned Lender shall account to Borrower for the shortfall; and

(d) Lender shall account to Borrower for the total costs and expenses incurred by Borrower as a result thereof as set out in paragraphs 9.3 and 9.4 from the time the notice is effective.

9.3 **Failure by either Party to redeliver**

This provision applies in the event that a Party (the "**Transferor**") fails to meet a redelivery obligation within the standard settlement time for the asset concerned on the exchange or in the clearing organisation through which the asset equivalent to the asset concerned was originally delivered or within such other period as may be agreed between the Parties. In such situation, in addition to the Parties' rights under the general law and this Agreement where the other Party (the "**Transferee**") incurs interest, overdraft or similar costs and expenses the Transferor agrees to pay on demand and hold harmless the Transferee with respect to all such costs and expenses which arise directly from such failure excluding (i) such costs and expenses which arise from the negligence or wilful default of the Transferee and (ii) any indirect or consequential losses. It is agreed by the Parties that any costs reasonably and properly incurred by a Party arising in respect of the failure of a Party to meet its obligations under a transaction to sell or deliver securities resulting from the failure of the Transferor to fulfil its redelivery obligations is to be treated as a direct cost or expense for the purposes of this paragraph.

9.4 **Exercise of buy-in on failure to redeliver**

In the event that as a result of the failure of the Transferor to fulfil its redelivery obligations a "buy-in" is exercised against the Transferee, then the Transferor shall account to the Transferee for the total costs and expenses reasonably incurred by the Transferee as a result of such "buy-in."

10 **SET-OFF ETC.**

10.1 **Definitions for paragraph 10**

In this paragraph 10:

"**Bid Price**" in relation to Equivalent Securities or Equivalent Collateral means the best available bid price on the most appropriate market in a standard size;

"**Bid Value**" subject to paragraph 10.5 means:

(a) in relation to Collateral equivalent to Collateral in the form of a Letter of Credit zero and in relation to Cash Collateral the amount of the currency concerned; and

(b) in relation to Equivalent Securities or Collateral equivalent to all other types of Collateral the amount which would be received on a sale of such Equivalent Securities or Equivalent Collateral at the Bid Price at Close of Business on the relevant Business Day less all costs, fees and expenses that would be incurred in connection therewith, calculated on the assumption that the aggregate thereof is the least that could reasonably be expected to be paid in order to carry out such sale or realisation and adding thereto the amount of any interest, dividends, distributions or other amounts, in the case of Equivalent Securities, paid to Borrower and in respect of which equivalent amounts have not been paid to Lender and in the case of Equivalent Collateral, paid to Lender and in respect of which equivalent amounts have not been paid to Borrower, in accordance with paragraph 6.1 prior to such time in respect of such Equivalent Securities, Equivalent Collateral or the original Securities or Collateral held, gross of all and any tax deducted or paid in respect thereof;

"**Offer Price**" in relation to Equivalent Securities or Equivalent Collateral means the best available offer price on the most appropriate market in a standard size;

"**Offer Value**" subject to paragraph 10.5 means:

(a) in relation to Collateral equivalent to Collateral in the form of a Letter of Credit zero and in relation to Cash Collateral the amount of the currency concerned; and

(b) in relation to Equivalent Securities or Collateral equivalent to all other types of Collateral the amount it would cost to buy such Equivalent Securities or Equivalent Collateral at the Offer Price at Close of Business on the relevant Business Day together with all costs, fees and expenses that would be incurred in connection therewith, calculated on the assumption that the aggregate thereof is the least that could reasonably be expected to be paid in order to carry out the transaction and adding thereto the amount of any interest, dividends, distributions or other amounts, in the case of Equivalent Securities, paid to Borrower and in respect of which equivalent amounts have not been paid to Lender and in the case of Equivalent Collateral, paid to Lender and in respect of which equivalent amounts have not been paid to Borrower, in accordance with paragraph 6.1 prior to such time in respect of such Equivalent Securities, Equivalent Collateral or the original Securities or Collateral held, gross of all and any tax deducted or paid in respect thereof;

10.2 **Termination of delivery obligations upon Event of Default**

Subject to paragraph 9, if an Event of Default occurs in relation to either Party, the Parties' delivery and payment obligations (and any other obligations they have under this Agreement) shall be accelerated so as to require performance thereof at the time such Event of Default occurs (the date of which shall be the "**Termination Date**" for the purposes of this clause) so that performance of such delivery and payment obligations shall be effected only in accordance with the following provisions:

(i) the Relevant Value of the securities which would have been required to be delivered but for such termination (or payment to be made, as the case may be) by each Party shall be established in accordance with paragraph 10.3; and

(ii) on the basis of the Relevant Values so established, an account shall bc taken (as at the Termination Date) of what is due from each Party to the other and (on the basis that each Party's claim against the other in respect of delivery of Equivalent Securities or Equivalent Collateral or any cash payment equals the Relevant Value thereof) the sums due from one Party shall be set-off against the sums due from the other and only the balance of the account shall be payable (by the Party having the claim valued at the lower amount pursuant to the foregoing) and such balance shall be payable on the Termination Date.

If the Bid Value is greater than the Offer Value, and the Non-Defaulting Party had delivered to the Defaulting Party a Letter of Credit, the Defaulting Party shall draw on the Letter of Credit to the extent of the balance due and shall subsequently redeliver for cancellation the Letter of Credit so provided.

If the Offer Value is greater than the Bid Value, and the Defaulting Party had delivered to the Non-Defaulting Party a Letter of Credit, the Non-Defaulting Party shall draw on the Letter of Credit to the extent of the balance due and shall subsequently redeliver for cancellation the Letter of Credit so provided.

In all other circumstances, where a Letter of Credit has been provided to a Party, such Party shall redeliver for cancellation the Letter of Credit so provided.

10.3 **Determination of delivery values upon Event of Default**

For the purposes of paragraph 10.2 the "**Relevant Value**":

(i) of any securities to be delivered by the Defaulting Party shall, subject to paragraph 10.5 below, equal the Offer Value of such securities; and

(ii) of any securities to be delivered to the Defaulting Party shall, subject to paragraph 10.5 below, equal the Bid Value of such securities.

10.4 For the purposes of paragraph 10.3, but subject to paragraph 10.5, the Bid Value and Offer Value of any securities shall be calculated for securities of the relevant description (as determined by the Non-Defaulting Party) as of the first Business Day following the Termination Date, or if the relevant Event of Default occurs outside the normal business hours of such market, on the second Business Day following the Termination Date (the "**Default Valuation Time**");

10.5 Where the Non-Defaulting Party has following the occurrence of an Event of Default but prior to the close of business on the fifth Business Day following the Termination Date purchased securities forming part of the same issue and being of an identical type and description to those to be delivered by the Defaulting Party or sold securities forming part of the same issue and being of an identical type and description to those to be delivered by him to the Defaulting Party, the cost of such purchase or the proceeds of such sale, as the case may be, (taking into account all reasonable costs, fees and expenses that would be incurred in connection therewith) shall (together with any amounts owing pursuant to paragraph 6.1) be treated as the Offer Value or Bid Value, as the case may be, of the amount of securities to be delivered which is equivalent to the amount of the securities so bought or sold, as the case may be, for the purposes of this paragraph 10, so that where the amount of securities to be delivered is more than the amount so bought or sold as the case may be, the Offer Value or Bid Value as the case may be, of the balance shall be valued in accordance with paragraph 10.4.

10.6 Any reference in this paragraph 10 to securities shall include any asset other than cash provided by way of Collateral.

10.7 **Other costs, expenses and interest payable in consequence of an Event of Default**

The Defaulting Party shall be liable to the Non-Defaulting Party for the amount of all reasonable legal and other professional expenses incurred by the Non-Defaulting Party in connection with or as a consequence of an Event of Default, together with interest thereon at the one-month London Inter Bank Offered Rate as quoted on a reputable financial information service ("**LIBOR**") as of 11.00 am, London Time, on the date on which it is to be determined or, in the case of an expense attributable to a particular transaction and where the parties have previously agreed a rate of interest for the transaction, that rate of interest if it is greater than LIBOR. The rate of LIBOR applicable to each month or part thereof that any sum payable pursuant to this paragraph 10.7 remains outstanding is the rate of LIBOR determined on the first Business Day of any such period of one month or any part thereof. Interest will accrue daily on a compound basis and will be calculated according to the actual number of days elapsed.

11. TRANSFER TAXES

Borrower hereby undertakes promptly to pay and account for any transfer or similar duties or taxes chargeable in connection with any transaction effected pursuant to or contemplated by this Agreement, and shall indemnify and keep indemnified Lender against any liability arising as a result of Borrower's failure to do so.

12. LENDER'S WARRANTIES

Each Party hereby warrants and undertakes to the other on a continuing basis to the intent that such warranties shall survive the completion of any transaction contemplated herein that, where acting as a Lender:

(a) it is duly authorised and empowered to perform its duties and obligations under this Agreement;

(b) it is not restricted under the terms of its constitution or in any other manner fron lending Securities in accordance with this Agreement or from otherwise performing its obligations hereunder;

(c) it is absolutely entitled to pass full legal and beneficial ownership of all Securities provided by it hereunder to Borrower free from all liens, charges and encumbrances; and

(d) it is acting as principal in respect of this Agreement or, subject to paragraph 16, as agent and the conditions referred to in paragraph 16.2 will be fulfilled in respect of any Loan which it makes as agent.

13. BORROWER'S WARRANTIES

Each Party hereby warrants and undertakes to the other on a continuing basis to the intent that such warranties shall survive the completion of any transaction contemplated herein that, where acting as a Borrower:

(a) it has all necessary licenses and approvals, and is duly authorised and empowered, to perform its duties and obligations under this Agreement and will do nothing prejudicial to the continuation of such authorisation, licences or approvals;

(b) it is not restricted under the terms of its constitution or in any other manner from borrowing Securities in accordance with this Agreement or from otherwise performing its obligations hereunder;

(c) it is absolutely entitled to pass full legal and beneficial ownership of all Collateral provided by it hereunder to Lender free from all liens, charges and encumbrances: and

(d) it is acting as principal in respect of this Agreement.

14. EVENTS OF DEFAULT

14.1 Each of the following events occurring in relation to either Party (the "**Defaulting Party**", the other Party being the "**Non-Defaulting Party**") shall be an Event of Default for the purpose of paragraph 10 but only (subject to sub-paragraph (v) below) where the Non-Defaulting Party serves written notice on the Defaulting Party:

(i) Borrower or Lender failing to pay or repay Cash Collateral or deliver Collateral or redeliver Equivalent Collateral or Lender failing to deliver Securities upon the due date;

(ii) Lender or Borrower failing to comply with its obligations under paragraph 5;

(iii) Lender or Borrower failing to comply with its obligations under paragraph 6.1;

(iv) Borrower failing to comply with its obligations to deliver Equivalent Securities in accordance with paragraph 8;

(v) an Act of Insolvency occurring with respect to Lender or Borrower, an Act of Insolvency which is the presentation of a petition for winding up or any analogous proceeding or the appointment of a liquidator or analogous officer of the Defaulting Party not requiring the Non-Defaulting Party to serve written notice on the Defaulting Party;

(vi) any representation or warranty made by Lender or Borrower being incorrect or untrue in any material respect when made or repeated or deemed to have been made or repeated;

(vii) Lender or Borrower admitting to the other that it is unable to, or it intends not to, perform any of its obligations under this Agreement and/or in respect of any Loan;

(viii) Lender (if applicable) or Borrower being declared in default or being suspended or expelled from membership of or participation in, any securities exchange or association or suspended or prohibited from dealing in securities by any regulatory authority;

(ix) any of the assets of Lender or Borrower or the assets of investors held by or to the order of Lender or Borrower being transferred or ordered to be transferred to a trustee (or a person exercising similar functions) by a regulatory authority pursuant to any securities regulating legislation, or

(x) Lender or Borrower failing to perform any other of its obligations under this Agreement and not remedying such failure within 30 days after the Non-Defaulting Party serves written notice requiring it to remedy such failure.

14.2 Each Party shall notify the other (in writing) if an Event of Default or an event which, with the passage of time and/or upon the serving of a written notice as referred to above, would be an Event of Default, occurs in relation to it.

14.3 The provisions of this Agreement constitute a complete statement of the remedies available to each Party in respect of any Event of Default.

14.4 Subject to paragraph 9.3 and 10.7, neither Party may claim any sum by way of consequential loss or damage in the event of failure by the other party to perform any of its obligations under this Agreement.

15. INTEREST ON OUTSTANDING PAYMENTS

In the event of either Party failing to remit sums in accordance with this Agreement such Party hereby undertakes to pay to the other Party upon demand interest (before as well as after judgment) on the net balance due and outstanding, for the period commencing on and inclusive of the original due date for payment to (but excluding) the date of actual payment, in the same currency as the principal sum and at the rate referred to in paragraph 10.7. Interest will accrue daily on a compound basis and will be calculated according to the actual number of days elapsed.

16. TRANSACTIONS ENTERED INTO AS AGENT

16.1 Power for Lender to enter into Loans as agent

Subject to the following provisions of this paragraph, Lender may (if so indicated in paragraph 6 of the Schedule) enter into Loans as agent (in such capacity, the "**Agent**") for a third person (a "**Principal**"), whether as custodian or investment manager or otherwise (a Loan so entered into being referred to in this paragraph as an "**Agency Transaction**").

16.2 Conditions for agency loan

A Lender may enter into an Agency Transaction if, but only if:

(i) it specifies that Loan as an Agency Transaction at the time when it enters into it;

(ii) it enters into that Loan on behalf of a single Principal whose identity is disclosed to Borrower (whether by name or by reference to a code or identifier which the Parties have agreed will be used to refer to a specified Principal) at the time when it enters into the Loan or as otherwise agreed between the Parties; and

(iii) it has at the time when the Loan is entered into actual authority to enter into the Loan and to perform on behalf of that Principal all of that Principal's obligations under the agreement referred to in paragraph 16.4(ii).

16.3 **Notification by Lender of certain events affecting the principal**

Lender undertakes that, if it enters as agent into an Agency Transaction, forthwith upon becoming aware:

(i) of any event which constitutes an Act of Insolvency with respect to the relevant Principal; or

(ii) of any breach of any of the warranties given in paragraph 16.5 or of any event or circumstance which has the result that any such warranty would be untrue if repeated by reference to the then current facts;

it will inform Borrower of that fact and will, if so required by Borrower, furnish it with such additional information as it may reasonably request.

16.4 Status of agency transaction

(i) Each Agency Transaction shall be a transaction between the relevant Principal and Borrower and no person other than the relevant Principal and Borrower shall be a party to or have any rights or obligations under an Agency Transaction. Without limiting the foregoing, Lender shall not be liable as principal for the performance of an Agency Transaction, but this is without prejudice to any liability of Lender under any other provision of this clause; and

(ii) all the provisions of the Agreement shall apply separately as between Borrower and each Principal for whom the Agent has entered into an Agency transaction or Agency Transactions as if each such Principal were a party to a separate agreement with Borrower in all respects identical with this Agreement other than this paragraph and as if the Principal were Lender in respect of that agreement;

PROVIDED THAT

if there occurs in relation to the Agent an Event of Default or an event which would constitute an Event of Default if Borrower served written notice under any subclause of paragraph 14, Borrower shall be entitled by giving written notice to the Principal (which notice shall be validly given if given to Lender in accordance with paragraph 21) to declare that by reason of that event an Event of Default is to be treated as occurring in relation to the Principal. If Borrower gives such a notice then an Event of Default shall be treated as occurring in relation to the Principal at the time when the notice is deemed to be given; and

if the Principal is neither incorporated in nor has established a place of business in Great Britain, the Principal shall for the purposes of the agreement referred to in paragraph 16.4(ii) be deemed to have appointed as its agent to receive on its behalf service of process in the courts of England the Agent, or if the Agent is neither incorporated nor has established a place of business in Great Britain, the person appointed by the Agent for the purposes of this Agreement, or such other person as the Principal may from time to time specify in a written notice given to the other Party.

The foregoing provisions of this paragraph do not affect the operation of the Agreement as between Borrower and Lender in respect of any transactions into which Lender may enter on its own account as principal.

16.5 **Warranty of authority by Lender acting as agent**

Lender warrants to Borrower that it will, on every occasion on which it enters or purports to enter into a transaction as an Agency Transaction, have been duly authorised to enter into that Loan and perform the obligations arising under such transaction on behalf of the person whom it specifies as the Principal in respect of that transaction and to perform on behalf of that person all the obligations of that person under the agreement referred to in paragraph 16.4(ii).

17. **TERMINATION OF THIS AGREEMENT**

Each Party shall have the right to terminate this Agreement by giving not less than 15 Business Days' notice in writing to the other Party (which notice shall specify the date of termination) subject to an obligation to ensure that all Loans which have been entered into but not discharged at the time such notice is given are duly discharged in accordance with this Agreement.

18. **SINGLE AGREEMENT**

Each Party acknowledges that, and has entered into this Agreement and will enter into each Loan in consideration of and in reliance upon the fact that, all Loans constitute a single business and contractual relationship and are made in consideration of each other. Accordingly, each Party agrees:

(i) to perform all of its obligations in respect of each Loan, and that a default in the performance of any such obligations shall constitute a default by it in respect of all Loans; and

(ii) that payments, deliveries and other transfers made by either of them in respect of any Loan shall be deemed to have been made in consideration of payments, deliveries and other transfers in respect of any other Loan.

19. SEVERANCE

If any provision of this Agreement is declared by any judicial or other competent authority to be void or otherwise unenforceable, that provision shall be severed from the Agreement and the remaining provisions of this Agreement shall remain in full force and effect. The Agreement shall, however, thereafter be amended by the Parties in such reasonable manner so as to achieve as far as possible, without illegality, the intention of the Parties with respect to that severed provision.

20. SPECIFIC PERFORMANCE

Each Party agrees that in relation to legal proceedings it will not seek specific performance of the other Party's obligation to deliver or redeliver Securities, Equivalent Securities, Collateral or Equivalent Collateral but without prejudice to any other rights it may have.

21. NOTICES

21.1 Any notice or other communication in respect of this Agreement may be given in any manner set forth below to the address or number or in accordance with the electronic messaging system details set out in paragraph 4 of the Schedule and will be deemed effective as indicated:

(i) if in writing and delivered in person or by courier, on the date it is delivered;

(ii) if sent by telex, on the date the recipient's answerback is received;

(iii) if sent by facsimile transmission, on the date that transmission is received by a responsible employee of the recipient in legible form (it being agreed that the burden of proving receipt will be on the sender and will not be met by a transmission report generated by the sender's facsimile machine);

(iv) if sent by certified or registered mail (airmail, if overseas) or the equivalent (return receipt requested), on the date that mail is delivered or its delivery is attempted; or

(v) if sent by electronic messaging system, on the date that electronic message is received,

unless the date of that delivery (or attempted delivery) or the receipt, as applicable, is not a Business Day or that communication is delivered (or attempted) or received, as applicable, after the Close of Business on a Business Day, in which case that communication shall be deemed given and effective on the first following day that is a Business Day.

21.2 Either party may by notice to the other change the address, telex or facsimile number or electronic messaging system details at which notices or other communications are to be given to it.

22. **ASSIGNMENT**

Neither Party may charge assign or transfer all or any of its rights or obligations hereunder without the prior consent of the other Party.

23. **NON-WAIVER**

No failure or delay by either Party (whether by course of conduct or otherwise) to exercise any right, power or privilege hereunder shall operate as a waiver thereof nor shall any single or partial exercise of any right, power or privilege preclude any other or further exercise thereof or the exercise of any other right, power or privilege as herein provided.

24. **GOVERNING LAW AND JURISDICTION**

24.1 This Agreement is governed by, and shall be construed in accordance with, English law.

24.2 The courts of England have exclusive jurisdiction to hear and decide any suit, action or proceedings, and to settle any disputes, which may arise out of or in connection with this Agreement (respectively, "**Proceedings**" and "**Disputes**") and, for these purposcs. each party irrevocably submits to the jurisdiction of the courts of England.

24.3 Each party irrevocably waives any objection which it might at any time have to the courts of England being nominated as the forum to hear and decide any Proceedings and to settle any Disputes and agrees not to claim that the courts of England are not a convenient or appropriate forum.

24.4 Each of Party A and Party B hereby respectively appoints the person identified in paragraph 5 of the Schedule pertaining to the relevant Party as its agent to receive on its behalf service of process in the courts of England. If such an agent ceases to be an agent of Party A or party B, as the case may be, the relevant Party shall promptly appoint, and notify the other Party of the identity of its new agent in England.

25. **TIME**

Time shall be of the essence of the Agreement.

26. **RECORDING**

The Parties agree that each may record all telephone conversations between them.

27. **WAIVER OF IMMUNITY**

Each Party hereby waives all immunity (whether on the basis of sovereignty or otherwise) from jurisdiction, attachment (both before and after judgement) and execution to which it might otherwise be entitled in any action or proceeding in the courts of England or of any other country or jurisdiction relating in any way to this Agreement and agrees that it will not raise, claim or cause to be pleaded any such immunity at or in respect of any such action or proceeding.

28. **MISCELLANEOUS**

28.1 This Agreement constitutes the entire agreement and understanding of the Parties with respect to its subject matter and supersedes all oral communication and prior writings with respect thereto.

28.2 The Party (the "**Relevant Party**") who has prepared the text of this Agreement for execution (as indicated in paragraph 7 of the Schedule) warrants and undertakes to the other Party that such text conforms exactly to the text of the standard form Global Master Securities Lending Agreement posted by the International Securities Lenders Association on its website on [] 2000 except as notified by the Relevant Party to the other Party in writing prior to the execution of this Agreement.

28.3 No amendment in respect of this Agreement will be effective unless in writing (including a writing evidenced by a facsimile transmission) and executed by each of the Parties or confirmed by an exchange of telexes or electronic messages on an electronic messaging system.

28.4 The obligations of the Parties under this Agreement will survive the termination of any Loan.

28.5 The warranties contained in paragraphs 12, 13, 16 and 28.2 will survive termination of this Agreement for so long as any obligations of either of the Parties pursuant to this Agreement remain outstanding.

28.6 Except as provided in this Agreement, the rights, powers, remedies and privileges provided in this Agreement are cumulative and not exclusive of any rights, powers, remedies and privileges provided by law.

28.7 This Agreement (and each amendment in respect of it) may be executed and delivered in counterparts (including by facsimile transmission), each of which will be deemed an original.

28.8 A person who is not a party to this Agreement has no right under the Contracts (Rights of Third Parties) Act 1999 to enforce any terms of this Agreement, but this does not affect any right or remedy of a third party which exists or is available apart from that Act.

EXECUTED by the **PARTIES**

SIGNED BY	)
	)
DULY AUTHORISED FOR AND	)
ON BEHALF OF	)

SIGNED BY	)
DULY AUTHORISED FOR AND	)
ON BEHALF OF	)

SCHEDULE

1. **Collateral**

1.1 The securities, financial instruments and deposits of currency set out in thc table below with a cross marked next to them are acceptable forms of Collateral under this Agreement.

1.2 Unless otherwise agreed between the Parties, the Market Value of the Collateral delivered pursuant to paragraph 5 by Borrower to Lender under the terms and conditions of this Agreement shall on each Business Day represent not less than the Market Value of the Loaned Securities together with the percentage contained in the row of the table below corresponding to the particular form of Collateral, referred to in this Agreement as the "**Margin**".

Security/Financial Instrument/Deposit of Currency	**Mark "X" if acceptable form of Collateral**	**Margin (%)**

1.3 Basis of Margin Maintenance:

Paragraph 5.4 (aggregation) shall not apply* ☐

The assumption is that paragraph 5.4 (aggregation) applies unless the box is ticked.

1.4 Paragraph 5.6 (netting of obligations to deliver Collateral and redeliver Equivalent Collateral) shall not apply* ☐

If paragraph 5.4 applies, the assumption is that paragraph 5.6 (netting) applies unless the box is ticked.

2. **Base Currency**

The Base Currency applicable to this Agreement is

3. **Places of Business**

(See definition of Business Day.)

4. **Designated Office and Address for Notices**

(A) **Designated office of Party A:**

Address for notices or communications to Party A:

Address:

Attention:

Facsimile No:

Telephone No:

Electronic Messaging System Details:

(B) **Designated office of Party B:**

Address for notices or communications to Party B:

Address:

Attention:

Facsimile No:

Telephone No:

Electronic Messaging System Details:

5. (A) **Agent of Party A for Service of Process**

Name:

Address:

(B) **Agent of Party B for Service of Process**

Name:

Address:

6. **Agency**

– Paragraph 16 may apply to Party A* ☐

– Paragraph 16 may apply to Party B* ☐

7. **Party Preparing this Agreement**

Party A* ☐

Party B* ☐

Appendix C

Settlement procedures

Overseas settlement

International equity market securities and AIM securities

S050 Unless otherwise agreed prior to the time the transaction is effected, a transaction effected by a **member firm** in an **international equity market security** shall be settled in accordance with the rules and procedures of the clearing and settlement system used. Any special terms or conditions relating to the settlement of a transaction in an **international equity market security** shall be agreed at or prior to the time the transaction is effected, and shall be clearly stated and described as such on any confirmation of the trade. Partial settlement shall not be permitted without the prior agreement of both parties to the transaction. *(Formerly rule 3.24)*

Good delivery

S060 In order to ensure good delivery of an **international equity market security**, a **member firm** shall conform with the good delivery requirements of the clearing and settlement system used. The **member firm** causing erroneous or bad delivery shall be liable for the **counterparty's** costs for return or transfer of the security. *(Formerly rules 3.26 and 18.14)*

General rules

Time for settlement (S100-S104)

S100 Unless otherwise agreed with the **Exchange**, or in the case of the return of stock under a **lending arrangement**, if a **member firm** agrees a due date for settlement of an **on Exchange** transaction in a **domestic market security** or an **AIM security** later than **standard settlement**, that date must not be more than 25 days after the date of the transaction. *(Replaces rule 10.2(a))*

S101 A conditional transaction may nevertheless be dealt for settlement up to 10 days after the day on which the condition is fulfilled. *(Formerly rule 10.2b)*

S102 A **member firm** trading in an **order book security** by means other than the **order book** shall agree the settlement arrangements with its **counterparty** prior to the time the transaction is effected. Any special terms or conditions relating to the settlement of a transaction shall be agreed at or prior to execution and shall be clearly stated on any confirmation of the transaction. *(Formerly rule 10.2(e)(i))*

S103 If settlement is effected in physical form, a **member firm** shall conform with the applicable good delivery requirements of the relevant settlement mechanism. *(Formerly rule 10.2(e)(ii))*

<u>**Standard settlement**</u> (S120-S128)

Transactions for three day rolling settlement (S120-S121)

S120 Unless otherwise agreed, and subject to rule S125, a transaction in the following is due for settlement on the third day after the day on which the transaction was effected:

S120.1 a **domestic market security**; *(Replaces rule 10.5)*

S120.2 an **AIM security**; *(New Rule)*

S120.3 a registered **fixed interest security** of an issuer incorporated in the **United Kingdom**;

S120.4 a non-convertible **fixed interest security** which is maintained on a register in the **United Kingdom**; or

S120.5 a security dealt subject to accrued interest which is not **CREST** eligible. *(Formerly rule 10.4)*

S121 A transaction in a **domestic market security** automatically executed in the **Exchange trading system** is due for settlement on the third day after the day on which the transaction was effected. *(Replaces rule 10.2(d))*

Transactions for next day settlement (S125-S126)

S125 Unless otherwise agreed, a transaction in the following is due for settlement on the day after the day on which the transaction was effected in:

S125.1 securities dealt subject to accrued interest other than those in rule S120.5; and

S125.2 a new issue transferable by delivery of scrip or renounceable documents or their dematerialised equivalent. *(Formerly rule 10.3)*

S126 A **member firm** shall resolve any queries arising out of a transaction effected for settlement on the next day by 10.30 on the day after the day the transaction was effected. *(Formerly rule 8.5(d))*.

Transactions for other standard settlement periods (S128)

S128 Unless otherwise agreed, a transaction in the following is due for settlement in accordance with the standard settlement on the exchange on which the security has its **principal listing**:

S128.1 **international retail service securities** settled in **CDI** form.

Cash settlement (S130)

S130 A transaction effected "for cash" in the securities specified:

S130.1 in rule S120 is due for settlement on the day after the day on which the transaction was effected; or

S130.2 in rule S125 is due for settlement on the same day as the day on which the transaction was effected. *(Formerly rule 10.6)*

Mandatory settlement (S135-S138)

S135 The **Exchange** may prescribe that transactions meeting specified criteria shall be due for settlement no later than **standard settlement** (an earlier settlement due date will be permitted). *(Formerly rule 10.9(a)(part))*

When invoking rule S135, the Exchange will prescribe:

- *the affected security or securities;*
- *the minimum value and or size of transaction to which rule S135 applies; and*
- *the period during which rule S135 applies. (New guidance)*

The ***Exchange*** *will normally consider requests from* ***member firms*** *to apply rule S135 in respect of*

- *an open-priced primary offering of further shares in a* ***domestic market security****; or*
- *a secondary offer or sale of a* ***domestic market security****; or*
- *an announced intention to sell a* ***domestic market security****.*

S136 Transaction under rule S135 shall be for "guaranteed delivery", in accordance with rule S137. Failure to settle on the settlement due date will result in the **Exchange** imposing a **fixed penalty** against the selling **member firm**.

No ***member firm*** *shall split a transaction to avoid the provisions of this rule. (Formerly rule 10.9(a))*

The provisions of this rule shall also apply to every transaction effected with an ***equity inter dealer broker****. (Formerly rule 10.9(b) and (c))*

S137 A **member firm** shall only effect a transaction for guaranteed delivery where the security is readily available to the **member firm** at the time of trading. *(Formerly rule 2.34(a).)*

S138 Where transactions effected under rule S137 are to be settled in **CREST**, the **seller** shall raise the settlement priority of guaranteed delivery transactions within **CREST** above any transactions not dealt for guaranteed delivery due for settlement on the same day. *(Formerly rule 2.34(b).)*

Calls on partly-paid securities (S140)

S140 Unless otherwise agreed, where delivery of partly-paid securities has not been made prior to the last time for registration before the call payment date, the **seller** shall be obliged to pay the call and the **buyer** shall reimburse the **seller** upon delivery of the fully paid (or next instalment paid) securities. *(Formerly rule 10.12)*

Stamp duty (S150-S151)

S150 Where the **seller** has paid any stamp duty the **buyer** shall reimburse the **seller** unless the obligation falls by law upon the **seller**. *(Formerly rule 10.13)*

S151 Where the **seller** is to pay stamp duty a **buyer** shall inform the **seller** of any applicable concessionary stamp duty rates. *(Formerly rule 10.14)*

Closed registers of companies in liquidation (S160-S162)

S160 Where a register has been closed following liquidation, a buying **member firm** shall pay against delivery of the transfer and certificate, or certified transfer, provided that it is accompanied by an authorisation from the registered holder to the liquidator that the liquidator pay to the **buyer** or its **client** any return of capital. *(Formerly rule 10.16(a))*

S161 A **seller** who is unable to deliver the documentation under rule S160 may not require payment until completion of the winding-up, at which time any distribution by the liquidator shall be delivered to the **buyer**. *(Formerly rule 10.16(b))*

S162 Where settlement of a **central counterparty contract** cannot take place because of a court, administrative, or regulatory order, or because of an insolvency event affecting the issuer of such securities, such **central counterparty contracts** shall be settled in accordance with the **LCH rules**. *(New rule)*

Replacement of securities subject to disability (S170–172)

S170 Where a security is placed by operation of law under a disability that does not apply to all other securities of the same issue, the **seller** must replace that security with one that is not subject to that disability. *(Formerly rule 10.21)*

S171 Where the issuer of bearer securities, including renounceable documents, fails to meet its obligations in relation to a security but not in relation to other securities of the same issue, the seller shall replace that security with one in relation to which the issuer is prepared to meet its obligations. *(Formerly rule 10.22.)*

S172 In the event of a chain of transactions the **Exchange** may determine that the obligation in rules S170 or S171 applies to one or more parties to the exclusion of others. *(Formerly rule 10.23)*

Registration of securities delivered as residual (S180-S182)

S180 Except as provided for in rule S181, a **member firm** which has purchased securities, other than as part of a **riskless principal transaction**, either on its own behalf or on behalf of a **client**, must ensure that the securities received are duly registered prior to any subsequent delivery of those securities in settlement of a sold transaction. *(Formerly rule 10.29(a))*

S181 Rule S180 applies to **market makers** unless, within two days of receipt of the securities by a **market maker**, that recipient **market maker** onward delivers the securities or, submits the securities for splitting, to facilitate settlement of a sold transaction already dealt. *(Formerly rule 10.29(b))*

S182 Any **member firm** granted an exemption under rules S180 or S181 must state clearly on the stock transfer form or subsequent split transfer forms its name and the date of onward delivery. *(Formerly rule 10.29(c))*

Settlement agents (S190-S192)

S190 A **member firm** may act as a **model A firm** or **model B firm** with the prior written consent of the **Exchange** with regard to each firm to which it wishes to offer its services as such. *(Formerly rule 10.31)*

S191 **Member firms** must make their own arrangements for settling transactions in accordance with these rules and may, but are not obliged to, employ their **General Clearing Member** as a **settlement agent**. **Individual Clearing Members** may also use a separate **settlement agent**. *(Formerly rule 10.32(a))*

S192 For **central counterparty contracts**, notwithstanding the settlement arrangements, the **clearing member** clearing the transaction is responsible for ensuring that every **central counterparty contract** to which it is a party is settled. *(Formerly rule 10.32(b).)*

Dealing agents (S195)

S195 A **member firm** for whom a **dealing agent** is acting shall be responsible for ensuring that the transaction effected on its behalf by the **dealing agent** is reported and settled. *(Formerly Rule 2.25(c))*

Clearing

Clearing arrangements (S200-S202)

S200 Subject to compliance with **LCH rules** and rule S201:

S200.1 A **General Clearing Member** may clear with **LCH** its own transactions or the transactions of another **member firm**;

S200.2 An **Individual Clearing Member** may clear with **LCH** its own transactions only; *(Formerly rule 10.33)*

S200.3 A **Non Clearing Member** must have a clearing agreement in place with a **General Clearing Member** to clear its **central counterparty transactions** with **LCH**. *(New Rule)*

S201 A **clearing member** which deals both as **principal** and **agent** in respect of **central counterparty transactions** must use a separate **General Clearing Member** entity to clear its **agency** business. *(Formerly rule 10.34(a))*

S202 A **member firm** may use more than one **General Clearing Member** and still use one **recognised BIC** provided that each **General Clearing Member** only clears one type of the **member firm's** business, either **agency** or **principal**. For any other arrangement a **member firm** must have a separate **recognised BIC** for each **General Clearing Member** that clears its business. *(Formerly rule 10.34(b))*

Continuing suitability (S205)

S205 A **clearing member** must comply with **LCH rules** with regard to clearing **central counterparty contracts** at all times. *(Formerly rule 1.8(c))*

Termination of clearing services (S210)

S210 A pre-agreed person at a **General Clearing Member** must notify the **Exchange** by telephone (subject to subsequent written confirmation) prior to suspending its services as a **clearing member** to any **member firm**. *(Formerly rule 1.23(b)(part))*

*In this event, the **Exchange** shall, at an agreed time, or as soon as is reasonably practicable, suspend such **member firm** from submitting orders in relation to all **central counterparty securities**, and delete any existing orders of that **member firm** residing in the **Exchange trading system**. The **General Clearing Member** remains liable for all trades by such **member firm** pending completion of the order deletion process by the **Exchange**.*

Responsibility of clearing member (S220)

S220 Notwithstanding the settlement arrangements, for **central counterparty contracts**, the **clearing member** clearing the transaction remains responsible for ensuring that every **central counterparty contract** to which it is a party is settled. *(Formerly rule 1.36(b))*

Net settlements – partial deliveries (S230-S233)

S230 Partial performance of net settlement instructions created through the use of the **central counterparty netting service** ("partial performance of net settlements") from **LCH** will be treated as being pro rata performance of the underlying **central counterparty contracts** between **LCH** and the relevant **clearing member** and between the **General Clearing Member** and the **Non Clearing Member** where **LCH** is settling directly with the **Non Clearing Member** or its **settlement agent**. *(New rule)*

S231 It is for the **General Clearing Member** to agree with its **Non Clearing Members** on what basis it will determine settlement priority of the onward principal **central counterparty contracts** between the **General Clearing Member** and its **Non Clearing Members**, where **LCH** is not settling directly with the **Non Clearing Member** or its **settlement agent**. In the event of a default of the **General Clearing Member** or **Non Clearing Member** where partial performance of net settlements from **LCH** has not been allocated to the **Non Clearing Members** and the **default procedures** are invoked, the onward principal **central counterparty contracts** will be deemed as unsettled **relevant principal contracts**. *(New rule)*

S232 In the event of partial performance of net settlements between the **General Clearing Member** and the **Non Clearing Member** or its **settlement agent** (or directly from **LCH** to the **Non Clearing Member** or its **settlement agent** as in rule S230) resulting from agency transactions, the **General Clearing Member's** obligations to the **Non Clearing Member's customers** in respect of these **central counterparty contracts** shall be deemed to have been partially performed on a pro rata basis. If the **Non Clearing Member**, or its **settlement agent** does not allocate, or allocates on an alternative basis, then it shall be deemed to have been pro rata and it shall be a term of the central counterparty contract that it shall be deemed partially performed on this basis. *(New rule)*

RepoClear

S233 In the event of partial performance of a net settlement arising from **on Exchange** contracts cleared by **RepoClear**, the **LCH rules** will determine what proportion of each **on Exchange** contract has been performed. *(Rule added N28/02 – effective 5 August 2002)*

Inter-office delivery

Times for delivery (S250-S252)

S250 Unless otherwise agreed, a **member firm** shall only deliver securities to another **member firm** between 09.00 hours and 17.00 hours on a business day. *(Formerly rule 10.27(part))*

S251 In the case of **gilt-edged securities** the delivery time shall be agreed between the **member firms**. *(Formerly rule 10.27(part))*

S252 Unless otherwise agreed, a **member firm** shall deliver securities dealt for next day settlement, other than **gilt-edged securities**, not later than the following times:

S252.1 11.45 hours in the case of delivery to a **market maker** or **broker dealer** by a **member firm** not acting as a **market maker** or an **equity inter dealer broker**;

S252.2 12.15 hours in the case of delivery by a **market maker** to another **market maker** or an **equity inter dealer broker**;

S252.3 12.30 hours in the case of delivery to a **market maker** by an **equity inter dealer broker**; or

S252.4 13.00 hours in the case of delivery by a **market maker** to any **member firm** not acting as a **market maker** or as an **equity inter dealer broker**. *(Formerly rule 10.28)*

Inter-office payment (S255)

S255 Where a **member firm** requires payment in cleared or same day funds, it shall notify the buying **member firm** before 10.30 on the day of delivery. *(Formerly rule 10.11)*

Certified transfers (S260)

S260 The **buyer** of securities may refuse to pay for a transfer unaccompanied by the certificate unless, in the case of securities on a **United Kingdom** register, the transfer is certified by the issuer. *(Formerly rule 10.24)*

Bearer securities (S270-S290)

S270 When settling transactions in bearer securities or renounceable letters of allotment, a **member firm** shall keep a record of the number of the certificate or letter together with a record of the transaction. *(Formerly rule 10.30)*

Imperfect delivery of bearer securities (S275-S276)

S275 A buying **member firm** may only return a certificate which has been delivered in an imperfect condition, (materially torn or damaged, having a material part of the wording obliterated or with insufficient or irregular coupons), within eight days of its delivery. *(Formerly rule 10.25)*

S276 A **member firm** to which securities in **American form** are delivered may require the deliverer to satisfy it that the transfer is effective. A **member firm** may decline to accept delivery of such securities endorsed in blank. *(Formerly rule 10.26)*

Delivery of bearer securities without coupon before they are made ex coupon (S280)

S280 The delivery of bearer securities (other than securities normally dealt for next day settlement) without the coupon before they are made ex coupon is not good delivery. *(Formerly rule 10.40)*

Delivery of bearer securities made ex dividend on or before settlement due date (S285)

S285 Where bearer securities other than securities normally dealt for next day settlement are made ex dividend on or before the due date for settlement of a transaction, the seller shall deliver the securities ex the coupon and account to the buyer for the dividend paid net of income tax. *(Formerly rule 10.41)*

Delivery of 3.5% War Loan (S290)

S290 Where 3.5% War Loan in bearer form is sold cum dividend and delivered after the ex dividend date, the bonds shall be delivered without the coupon, and the dividend settled without deduction of tax. *(Formerly rule 10.50)*

Benefits

Entitlements and instruction notices (S300-S302)

S300 Except as specified in rule S331, a transaction in a security effected on a day (including a transaction effected before the **mandatory quote**

period) that the **Exchange** makes a security ex an entitlement or at any time thereafter, shall be settled ex that entitlement, unless otherwise agreed at the time of dealing. *(Formerly rule 10.36(a))*

S301 For the purposes of the **settlement procedures**, unless otherwise stated, any reference to an **instruction notice** being given to the **seller** shall, in relation to a benefit pertaining to a **central counterparty transaction**, be read as a reference to the **instruction notice** being submitted by the **matched buyer** via **CREST** within the **CREST instruction deadline**. *(Formerly rule 10.36(b))*

S302 **Buyers** giving instructions within the deadlines set out in the rules must ensure that the instruction is given in time for the **seller** to receive it by that deadline. *(Formerly rule 10.36(c))*

<u>**Valuation notices**</u> (S305-S310)

S305 Where new securities have not been delivered in settlement of a free of payment claim in a transferable security resulting from an **on Exchange** transaction which has settled, the **buyer** may give the **seller** notice in writing that the **seller** shall deliver the new securities, or pay the value thereof, by the close of business on the third business day after receipt of the valuation notice. Such notice may be given from the fourth day after the new securities have been made available by the issuer or its agent. The **seller** shall deliver the new securities, or pay their value as instructed. *(Formerly rule 10.36A)*

S306 Where a **seller**, having paid the value of the new securities, delivers all or some of them, the **buyer** shall repay the **seller** the value of the new securities in proportion to the securities delivered against a claim from the **seller**. *(Formerly rule 10.36B)*

Calculation of valuation amount (S310)

S310 The value of the new securities shall be calculated:

S310.1 by reference to the middle of the quotation shown on the Stock Exchange Daily Official List on the day the valuation notice is issued; or

S310.2 where there is no quotation shown on the Stock Exchange Daily Official List, on the opening price of the security obtained from the principal market on which it is dealt on the day the valuation notice is issued. *(Formerly rule 10.36C)*

Special Cum transactions (S320-S321)

S320 A **member firm** shall not **on Exchange** effect a special cum transaction on or after the payment date in the case of a cash benefit or on or after the distribution date in the case of a stock benefit. *(Formerly rule 10.37(a))*

S321 A **member firm** shall not **on Exchange** make up a cum dividend transaction in a **gilt-edged security** with an ex dividend transaction in that security. *(Formerly rule 10.37(e))*

Special Ex transactions (S330-S334)

S330 A **member firm** shall not **on Exchange** effect a special ex transaction in a **gilt-edged security**. *(Formerly rule 10.37(b)(i))*

S331 A transaction in a **gilt-edged security** or **fixed interest security** due to be settled subsequent to the date on which the **Exchange** makes that security ex an entitlement, shall be dealt ex that entitlement unless otherwise agreed at the time of dealing. *(Formerly rule 10.44)*

S332 A **member firm** shall not **on Exchange** effect a special ex transaction in a **listed** fixed interest non-convertible security issued by a **United Kingdom** incorporated company or maintained on a register in the **United Kingdom** earlier than seven calendar days before the ex date. *(Formerly rule 10.37(b)(ii))*

S333 A **member firm** shall not **on Exchange** effect a special ex transaction in a security registered in the **United Kingdom** other than a security falling within rules S320 or S322 earlier than the tenth day before the ex date. *(Formerly rule 10.37(b)(iii))*

S334 A **member firm** shall not **on Exchange** effect a transaction in a traditional option for the put or call or both in a security on an ex basis before the ex date of that security. *(Formerly rule 10.37(c))*

Dividend strips (S340)

S340 A **member firm** shall not **on Exchange** effect a transaction in prospective dividends. *(Formerly rule 10.37(d))*

Special transactions (S350-S351)

S350 Where an **on Exchange** transaction is effected for settlement in the **United Kingdom**, is not for cash and the settlement due date is not one which, in accordance with rules S100 to S130, applies in default of any contrary agreement, the transaction shall be reported to the **Exchange** using the "SP" trade reporting condition if that non-standard settlement date has affected the price. *(Formerly rule 10.38(a))*

S351 Where a **domestic market security**, an **international equity market security** or a **fixed interest security** or an **AIM security** bought cum dividend **on Exchange** is to be made ex dividend on or before the settlement date of the transaction, a **buyer** who requires delivery of the coupon or the sterling value of the coupon without deduction of income tax shall effect a special transaction. Where the value of the coupon is disputed, its value shall be fixed by the **Exchange**. *(Formerly rule 10.38(b))*

Overseas securities (S360-S362)

S360 For the purposes of the **settlement procedures**, **overseas** securities shall not be treated as such if they are also **central counterparty securities**. *(Formerly rule 10.39(a))*

S361 A **member firm** shall treat **overseas** securities whose **principal listing** is not on the **Exchange** as being ex a benefit from the time they are marked ex that benefit on the home exchange, unless otherwise agreed. *(Formerly rule 10.39(b))*

S362 Where an **overseas** registered security is delivered more than 15 calendar days before the last day on which transfers will be accepted for registration cum the benefit of any entitlement, a **buyer** who fails to register shall not have a claim against the **seller** for that benefit. *(Formerly rule 10.42)*

Foreign currency valuations (S370)

S370 Where a security has been sold and a benefit or its cash equivalent is to be paid to holders of the security in a foreign currency, but it is agreed that the **seller** shall account for it in sterling, then unless otherwise agreed, the conversion rate in respect of the benefit shall be the closing mid-price spot rate on the day the benefit is due. *(Formerly rule 10.43)*

Dividends

Payment of dividends (S400-S401)

S400 Subject to rule S362, the **seller** is responsible for any dividend due to the buyer unless:

S400.1 an unreasonable time has been taken by the transferee in the execution and lodgment of the documents for registration; or

S400.2 there has been a delay of more than six months from the record date or three months from the pay date (whichever is the later) in claiming the dividend. After this time the **seller** must use reasonable endeavours to obtain the dividend from their **client** on behalf of the **buyer**. *(Formerly rule 10.45)*

Currency for dividend payments (S401)

S401 Unless otherwise agreed at the time of the transaction, dividends shall be payable in the same currency as that paid by the issuer. *(Formerly rule 18.16)*

Settlement of dividend claims (S405)

S405 A dividend claim made by one **member firm** to another and not disputed shall be settled not later than 28 calendar days after receipt of the claim or 14 calendar days after the payment date, whichever is the later. *(Formerly rule 10.46)*

Dividends with alternatives (S410)

S410 Except in the case of overseas securities and **central counterparty transactions**, where a company declares a dividend with one or more alternatives, a **buyer** wishing to opt for an alternative shall give the **seller** an **instruction notice** stating the form in which it requires the dividend:

S410.1 if the **seller** is acting as **agent**, not later than three days before the last date given by the company for accepting an alternative; or

S410.2 if the **seller** is acting as **principal** not later than four days before the last date given by the company for accepting an alternative. *(Formerly rule 10.47)*

Deduction of dividends (S415)

S415 Where the **seller** delivers securities direct to the **buyer**, the **buyer** may deduct a dividend to which it is entitled from payment if delivery is made after the last day on which transfers are accepted for registration cum dividend. *(Formerly rule 10.48)*

Cancellation of dividends (S420)

S420 On receipt of information cancelling or deferring the recommendation or declaration of a dividend, the **Exchange** may issue a **notice** cancelling the ex action and, as a result:

S420.1 any **notice** published making the security ex dividend is automatically cancelled and devoid of effect;

S420.2 any document issued by the **Exchange** in respect of a cancelled dividend is automatically withdrawn and devoid of effect;

S420.3 a transaction effected ex dividend, other than a transaction effected special ex dividend, shall not be adjusted;

S420.4 a transaction effected special cum or special ex dividend shall be adjusted;

S420.5 the cash equivalent in respect of the cancelled dividend shall be refunded;

S420.6 the **seller** shall re-attach the coupon in respect of the dividend, in the case of a bearer certificate. *(Formerly rule 10.49)*

Traditional options (S430-S436)

Dividends (S430-S431)

S430 A **buyer** of securities arising from the exercise of a **traditional option** is entitled to a cash payment equivalent to any net dividend that may have accrued in respect of those securities from the day the **traditional option** was dealt to the day it was exercised. *(Formerly rule 10.51)*

S431 Where, upon the exercise of a **traditional option**, the underlying securities have been marked ex dividend after the declaration day applicable to the option, the **buyer** of the securities is entitled to the dividend and to claim a tax certificate. *(Formerly rule 10.52)*

Dividends with alternatives (S435-S436)

S435 Where a security on which a dividend has been declared in alternative forms is bought as a result of the exercise of a **traditional option**, the **buyer** is entitled to the dividend in an alternative form if:

S435.1 the option is exercised at least one day before the last time specified in rule S410; and

S435.2 the buyer notifies the deliverer in writing before the last time specified in rule S410 of the form in which the dividend is required. *(Formerly rule 10.53)*

S436 Where the conditions specified in rule S435 are not satisfied, the dividend shall be settled in the form in which it was declared. *(Formerly rule 10.54)*

Rights Issues

S500 Where the **call payment day** or **registration day** is not a **business day** the relevant day is the immediately preceding **business day**. *(Formerly rule 10.55)*

S501 In relation to transactions in **overseas** securities where the transaction is to be settled in the **United Kingdom**, the **last time for claims** shall be 16.00 and the latest times for deliveries shall be the **specified times** on the day five days earlier than the **call payment day** or **registration day** if there is, and eight days earlier if there is not, a London call payment agent. *(Formerly rule 10.56)*

Delivery in settlement of transactions in securities dealt cum rights (S505)

S505 In order to settle a transaction in securities dealt cum rights where **rights** have already been issued, the seller shall deliver the **rights** by the **specified time** on the due date for settlement, but if the rights have not yet been issued the **seller** shall deliver them immediately when they become available. *(Formerly rule 10.57)*

Last time for issue of rights claims (S510-S511)

S510 A buyer that issues a claim to a seller to deliver **rights** or registered securities shall do so in writing not later than the **last time for claims** in order to become entitled to those **rights** or the new securities as the case may be. *(Formerly rule 10.58)*

S511 If the securities are to be settled through **CREST** a claim for the associated **rights** is not required, as a notification will be issued to a firm requiring that firm to deliver as specified. *(Formerly rule 10.59)*

Delivery in settlement of transactions in rights (S515)

S515 Except as is otherwise provided by these rules, where a **rights** offer is made by means of renounceable documents, the **rights** shall be delivered in settlement of a transaction through **CREST**, unless the parties agree that they shall be delivered in renounceable documents fully renounced. *(Formerly rule 10.60)*

Last times for delivery of rights (S520)

S520 A **seller** to whom a **rights** claim is issued shall deliver the **rights** at or before the **latest time for delivery** and a **buyer** is not obliged to accept delivery of **rights** after that time. *(Formerly rule 10.61)*

Obligations of seller where rights not delivered (S525-S526)

S525 Where nil paid or partly paid **rights** are not delivered by the **latest time for delivery**, the **seller** shall, unless a **lapsing instruction** has been given, make any payment due on the **call payment day** on behalf of the **buyer**. The **buyer** shall then refund to the **seller** the call payment against delivery of the paid up shares, or partly paid **rights**, as the case may be. *(Formerly rules 10.62 and 10.63)*

S526 Where fully paid **rights** are not delivered by the **latest time for delivery**:

S526.1 the **seller** shall deliver the registered securities to the **buyer**;

S526.2 the **seller** is liable for any additional duties or fees payable in order to comply with legislation; and

S526.3 if the securities are **CREST** eligible, the **seller** and the **buyer** shall immediately report the details of the transaction to **CREST**. *(Formerly rule 10.64)*

Late claims in respect of nil paid rights (S530-S531)

S530 Where a **buyer** issues a **rights** claim after the **last time for claims** but before the last time for acceptance of an offer, the **seller** shall, unless it has been able to prevent the rights lapsing, pay to the **buyer** an amount representing the lapsed rights premium, if any. *(Formerly rule 10.65)*

S531 Where a **buyer** issues a **rights** claim more than six months after the last time for acceptance of an offer, its claim shall be treated as invalid, and the selling firm shall not be required to make any payment to the buying firm in respect of the lapsed rights premium. *(Formerly rule 10.66)*

Late claims in respect of partly or fully paid rights (S535)

S535 Where a **buyer** issues a **rights** claim in respect of fully paid rights after the **last time for claims**, the **seller** shall deliver the registered securities, and the **buyer** is liable for any additional duties or fees payable in order to comply with legislation. *(Formerly rule 10.67)*

Lapsing instructions (S540-S543)

S540 Where a **buyer** does not receive full delivery of nil paid **rights** by the **latest time for delivery** it may at any time not later than 11.00 on the day before **call payment day** give the **seller** a **lapsing instruction**. *(Formerly rule 10.68)*

S541 Where a **lapsing instruction** is given orally, the **buyer** shall confirm it in writing by 12.00 on the day after the day on which the instruction was given. *(Formerly rule 10.69)*

S542 Where a **lapsing instruction** has been given and, if necessary, confirmed, delivery of the **rights** may be dispensed with by agreement. The delivery of the rights is dispensed with where the **lapsing instruction** is given via **CREST** in respect of a **central counterparty security**, as the bargain is automatically transformed in **CREST**. *(Formerly rule 10.70)*

S543 Notwithstanding that delivery is wholly or partly dispensed with, the **buyer** shall make payment in settlement of the transaction. *(Formerly rule 10.71)*

<u>**Payment of distribution to buyer**</u> (S545)

S545 Where a **lapsing instruction** has been given, the **seller** shall pay the **buyer** the amount representing the lapsed rights premium, if any. *(Formerly rule 10.72)*

<u>**Reference codes**</u> (S550)

S550 Where a **lapsing instruction** is given, the **member firms** concerned shall exchange the reference codes allocated by them to the transaction and any subsequent confirmation relating to that **lapsing instruction** shall incorporate both reference codes. *(Formerly rule 10.73)*

<u>**Rights issues and traditional options**</u> (S555)

S555 Where securities on which **traditional option** positions are open are made ex rights:

S355.1 where not otherwise agreed, an official valuation for the rights shall be fixed on application to the **Exchange**.

S355.2 rights in respect of traditional options shall be settled between the **counterparties** by the payment of an amount equal to the valuation fixed by the **Exchange**, unless otherwise agreed.

S355.3 the payment shall be made only where the option is exercised.

S355.4 the exercise price of the option shall remain unchanged. *(Formerly rule 10.74)*

Capitalisation issues

<u>Capitalisation claims</u>

S580 Where a **buyer** of securities cum capitalisation, or **CREST** on behalf of the **buyer**, makes a claim for the benefit of the capitalisation issue, the **member firm** against which the claim is made shall meet that claim by delivering the new securities to the claimant provided that:

S580.1 if the claim is against a **member firm** acting as principal:

(i) any part of the claim which is dependent upon a corresponding claim made by that firm against a **member firm** acting as agent, shall be delivered in settlement of the claim when and to the extent that the **member firm** acting as principal receives the shares or the proceeds of their sale in satisfaction of the corresponding claim; and

(ii) the claim shall be made within six years after delivery;

S580.2 where a claim against a **member firm** acting as agent is made later one year after delivery, the **member firm** may reject the claim if the client fails to deliver the shares or the proceeds of their sale; and

S580.3 if the claim is in respect of a transaction in an **overseas** registered security, rule S362 shall apply. *(Formerly rule 10.75)*

Claims for delivery of renounceable documents (S585-S586)

S585 Where a capitalisation issue is made by means of renounceable documents, unless delivery of the renounceable documents is agreed upon, a claim may be satisfied by delivery through **CREST** provided that claim is made more than:

S585.1 two days before the registration day; or

S585.2 where the renounceable documents will be registered on a register maintained outside the **United Kingdom**, ten days before the registration day. *(Formerly rule 10.76)*

S586 Where a claim for the delivery of renounceable documents has been made within the time specified in rule S585 but the **seller** delivers registered securities, the **seller** is liable for stamp duty (provided that the **buyer** has claimed any relief to which he is entitled from ad valorem stamp duty) and other charges that may arise from its failure to deliver in renounceable form. *(Formerly rule 10.77)*

Traditional options (S590)

S590 Where a security on which a **traditional option** position is open is made ex capitalisation, the option, if exercised, shall be settled by delivery of the new shares. *(Formerly rule 10.81)*

Entitlement issues

Application (S600-S601)

S600 Rules S600-S626 apply where securities are offered, by the issuer or a third party, to the holders of existing securities in proportion to their existing holdings by means of an assignable application form. *(Formerly rule 10.82)*

S601 Unless otherwise agreed, a **member firm** shall deal a security ex entitlement:

S601.1 as from the day of the announcement of an offer (including that day), if its full terms are published before 08:00;

S601.2 as from the day after the announcement (including that day), if its full terms are published after 08:00. *(Formerly rule 10.83)*

Entitlement claims (S605)

S605 Subject to S362, where a **buyer** of securities cum entitlement, or **CREST** on behalf of a **buyer**, makes a claim in writing for the assignment of the application form or the equivalent **uncertificated security** in favour of the **buyer** not later than 16.00 two days before the last day for acceptance, the **buyer** is entitled to receive the assigned application form. *(Formerly rule 10.84)*

Last times for delivery (S610)

S610 A **buyer** is not obliged to accept delivery of an assigned application form or the equivalent **uncertificated security** after the following times on the day before the closing of the offer:

S610.1 11.45 hours in the case of delivery to any **member firm** by a **member firm** acting as **agent**;

S610.2 12.15 hours in the case of delivery by a **member firm** acting as **principal** to a **member firm** acting as **principal**;

S610.3 12.30 hours in the case of delivery by an **equity inter dealer broker** to a **member firm** acting as **principal**;

S610.4 13.00 hours in the case of delivery by a **member firm** acting as **principal** to a **member firm** acting as **agent**; or

S610.5 in the case of a delivery to any **member firm** by means of delivery via **CREST**, by the final time for that type of delivery as specified in **CREST's** daily processing timetable. *(Formerly rule 10.85)*

Obligations of seller where application form not delivered (S615-S618)

S615 Where the assigned application form or the equivalent **uncertificated security** is not delivered by the time specified in rule S610, and unless a **lapsing instruction** is received from the **buyer** prior to 11.00 on the day before the **call payment date**, the **seller** shall take up the entitlement and deliver the new shares against payment of the application money. *(Formerly rule 10.86)*

S616 Where the new shares are **CREST** eligible securities the **seller** and the **buyer** shall at the earliest opportunity report the details of the transaction to **CREST** stating a maximum of three day settlement. *(Formerly rule 10.87)*

S617 The transaction shall be reported and matched for the value of the application money and for cash. *(Formerly rule 10.88)*

S618 Where new shares are delivered in accordance with rule S615, the **seller** is liable for any nominal stamp duty on the transfer, provided the **buyer** has claimed the appropriate relief. *(Formerly rule 10.89)*

Offers that do not become effective (S620)

S620 Where an offer does not become effective, a transaction effected ex entitlement shall be adjusted by the amount of a valuation fixed by the **Exchange**. *(Formerly rule 10.90)*

Traditional options (S626-S626)

S625 Where securities in respect of which option money has been given become the subject of an entitlement issue the option holder may claim the securities provided that the option is exercised not later than two days before the last date for application. Entitlements may be split if required. *(Formerly rule 10.91(a))*

S626 Any claim under rule S625 shall be irrevocable. *(Formerly rule 10.91(b))*

Conversions and drawings

Buyer's instructions to seller where delivery not received (S650-S652)

S650 Unless otherwise agreed at the time of dealing, a **buyer** of convertible securities or **warrants**, or both, cum the right to subscribe for or convert into another security who has not received delivery four days before the last day on which the rights can next be exercised shall, subject to rules S660 and S661, give the **seller** notice in writing of how the rights are to be exercised. *(Formerly rule 10.92)*

S651 A **seller** to whom notice is given under rules S660 or S665 shall exercise the rights in accordance with the **buyer's** instructions. *(Formerly rule 10.93)*

S652 The **buyer** shall refund the **seller** any subscription or conversion premiums incurred. *(Formerly rule 10.94)*

Last times for issue of conversion instructions (S660-S661)

S660 For any **instruction notice**, other than in a **central counterparty security** the **buyer** shall give the **seller** an **instruction notice** of how the rights are to be exercised by the following times:

S660.1 13.00 hours, four days before the last day where the **buyer** is not a **principal**, an **equity inter dealer broker**, a **gilt inter dealer broker** or a **wholesale dealer broker**; or

S660.2 10.00 hours, three days before the last day, where the **buyer** is a **principal**, or an **equity inter dealer broker**, a **gilt inter dealer broker** or a **wholesale dealer broker**. *(Formerly rule 10.95(a))*

S661 For **instruction notices** in **central counterparty securities** and for voluntary events in **central counterparty securities** where the intended settlement date of the transaction was on or before the date of the **CREST instruction deadline** and delivery did not take place, the **buyer** shall give the **seller** an **instruction notice** of how the rights are to be exercised by the **CREST instruction deadline**. *(Formerly rule 10.95(b))*

Drawn securities (S665)

S665 Unless a transaction in redeemable securities has been dealt for guaranteed delivery with a settlement due date prior to the drawing in question, a **buyer** shall, if the securities in question have been drawn since the transaction was dealt, accept from the **seller** the drawing payment in place of the drawn securities in settlement of the transaction. *(Formerly rule 10.96)*

Takeovers

Transactions in assented shares (S700)

S700 Where a transaction is dealt in assented shares, the delivery of unassented shares accompanied by a form of assent is not good delivery. *(Formerly rule 10.97)*

Delivery of unassented shares or the result of an offer (S710-S712)

S710 A **buyer** may give an **instruction notice**, specifying the offer to which it relates, to the **seller** requiring delivery of:

S710.1 the unassented shares at a date which is not later than the close of business two days before the next closing date; or

S710.2 the result of an offer or a specified election under the terms of the offer if the offer should become unconditional in all respects. *(Formerly rule 10.98)*

S711 The **seller** shall deliver the unassented shares or the result as instructed, if:

S711.1 the case of any **instruction notice**, other than those in a **central counterparty security**, the instruction was received no later than three (or, in the case of a selling principal four)

days before the next closing date in the case of a specified election; or

S711.2 for **instruction notices** in **central counterparty securities**, the instruction was received by the **seller** before the **CREST instruction deadline** and, for voluntary events in **central counterparty securities**, where the intended settlement date of the transaction was on or before the date of the **CREST instruction deadline** and delivery did not take place. *(Formerly rule 10.99)*

S712 If the **buyer** has paid the **seller** in advance of delivery and the **seller** fails to deliver the result of the offer or specified election by the day following the day on which the **buyer** would have received the results of the offer (had the non-assented shares been delivered to the **buyer** in sufficient time for them to elect or be on the register in their own right), the **seller** shall reimburse the **buyer** on that day an amount of money equal to the original bargain consideration. *(Formerly rule 10.100)*

Benefits in takeovers (S720-S721)

S720 Any transaction which is assented to the terms of a takeover offer shall (subject to the offer becoming unconditional in all respects) be dealt cum all benefits due in respect of the target security unless otherwise agreed at the time of dealing. *(Formerly rule 10.101)*

S721 For the purposes of this section on takeovers, references to:

S721.1 the final announcement date mean in respect of any offer, the date on which the final closing date for that offer is announced;

S271.2 the final closing date mean in respect of any offer, the date specified on the final announcement date as being the date on which that offer closes and, except in respect of a compulsory acquisition, for which there is no extension;

S721.3 offer shall be read so as to include any extended offer, election or extended election. *(Formerly rule 10.102)*

Stock situations (other than conversions and takeovers)

Delivery of unassented shares or the result of a stock situation (S750-S752)

S750 In **stock situations** other than conversions or takeovers a **buyer** may give an **instruction notice** specifying the option to which it relates, to the **seller** requiring delivery of:

S750.1 the unassented shares at a date which is not later than two days before the final election date, or final registration date whichever is the earlier; or

S750.2 the result of a **stock situation** or a specified election under the terms of the **stock situation** if it becomes effective. *(Formerly rule 10.103)*

S751 In the case of any **instruction notice**, other than those in a **central counterparty security**, the **seller** shall deliver the unassented shares or the result as instructed if the instruction was received no later than three (or, in the case of a selling principal, four) days before;

S751.1 the final election date in the case of a specified election;

S751.2 the final registration date in the case of delivery of underlying shares if that is prior to the election date. *(Formerly rule 10.104(a))*

S752 For **instruction notices** in **central counterparty securities** the **seller** shall deliver the unassented shares or the result as instructed if the **instruction** was received by the **seller** before the **CREST instruction deadline** and, for voluntary events in **central counterparty securities**, where the intended settlement date of the transaction was on or before the date of the **CREST instruction deadline** and delivery did not take place. *(Formerly rule 10.104(b))*

Delivery of results for non-optional events (S760-S761)

S760 Where the **seller** fails to deliver securities as traded, prior to the last time for registration in a non optional **stock situation** (such as a consolidation, subdivision, redemption, scheme and other **stock situations** where the holder of the securities has no option as to whether or not to participate), and the **buyer** has not given instructions to elect for any alternatives which may be available, the **seller** shall be obliged to deliver the results of the event against an amount of money equal to the original bargain consideration. *(Formerly rule 10.105)*

S761 If the **buyer** has paid the **seller** in advance of delivery and the **seller** fails to deliver the result of the event or specified election by the day following the day on which the **buyer** would have received the results of the event (had the underlying securities been delivered to the **buyer** in sufficient time for them to elect or be on the register in their own right), the **seller** shall reimburse the **buyer** on that day an amount of money equal to the original bargain consideration. *(Formerly rule 10.106)*

Buying-In

Request to buy-in (S800-S807)

S800 In accordance with timescales published by the **Exchange** from time to time, a **member firm** may request that the **Exchange** buy-in securities which have not been delivered in settlement of an **on Exchange** transaction. *(Formerly rule 12.2(part))*

S801 The **requesting party** must submit its **buying-in** request to the Buying-In Office at the **Exchange** in the prescribed form. *(Formerly rule 12.2(b))*

S802 A **buying-in** request received by the Buying-In Office after 14.00 hours is deemed to be received on the next day. *(Formerly rule 12.2(b))*

S803 A **buying-in** request in respect of a **central counterparty transaction** may only be made against any resultant settlement instructions. *(New rule)*

Withdrawal of a buying-in request (S805-S807)

S805 If the **requesting party** wishes to withdraw its **buying-in** request, it must instruct the Buying-In Office, in the manner prescribed by the **Exchange**. This procedure must also be followed if the **liable party** settles the original transaction before the deadline set by the **Exchange**. *(Formerly rule 12.3(a))*

S806 The **requesting party** must accept and pay for any securities delivered by the **Exchange** that result from a **buying-in** transaction where the **requesting party** has failed to withdraw the **buying-in** request before the deadline set by the **Exchange**. *(Formerly rule 12.3(b))*

S807 The **requesting party** cannot withdraw a **buying-in** request in respect of a **central counterparty transaction**, and will not be required to accept delivery where settlement of the transaction in respect of which it has issued the **buying-in** request has already occurred. *(New rule))*

Suspension of buying-in (S810)

S810 The **Exchange** may, at its discretion, suspend, postpone (either for a defined period or indefinitely) or cancel the **buying-in** of securities at any time, either generally, or in relation to a particular **member firm**, or a particular security. *(Formerly rule 12.4)*

Buying-in notice (S820-S830)

S820 The **Exchange** will issue a **buying-in notice** to the **liable party** on the same day (established in accordance with rule S800.2) as it receives a **buying-in** request specifying:

S820.1 details of the transaction in respect of which the **buying-in notice** is issued; and

S820.2 the date it intends to take **buying-in** action. *(Formerly rule 12.5(a))*

S821 The **Exchange** may buy-in undelivered securities on or after the sixth day after receipt of a **buying-in** request relating to those securities except for transactions dealt for guaranteed delivery where the **Exchange** may immediately buy-in the undelivered securities on receipt of a **buying-in** request. *(Formerly rule 12.5(b))*

S822 For transactions dealt for guaranteed delivery the **liable party** might not receive prior notification from the **Exchange** of the **buying-in** action. *(Formerly rule 12.3(c))*

Passing on of buying-in notices (S830)

S830 Except for transactions dealt for guaranteed delivery, a **member firm** in receipt of a **buying-in notice** for a transaction in which it acted as **principal** may, at any time up to 14:00 hours two days before the **buying-in** date, either:

S830.1 nominate in its place one or more transactions in securities of the same description to which it is a **buyer** and for which settlement has been outstanding for the longest period; or

S830.2 nominate in its place the **member firm** which is the **seller** in an **across principal closing** or **riskless principal transaction**.

S830.3 A nomination made pursuant to this rule may only be withdrawn once the original transaction is settled or at the instigation of the **member firm** which gave the original **buying-in** request. *(Formerly rule 12.6)*

Settlement of buying-in transactions (S840-S843)

S840 Where the **Exchange** executes a trade to purchase securities for delivery to the **liable party** to satisfy a **buying-in notice**, it will deal for:

S840.1 two day settlement for a **CREST** eligible security;

S840.2 four day settlement for any other security; or

S840.3 at the **Exchange's** discretion, any other settlement period. *(Formerly rule 12.7)*

S841 The **Exchange** shall notify the **liable party** of the details of the **buying-in** transaction following which the **liable party** must immediately match a delivery instruction with the **Exchange** in **CREST** or in such other settlement system as notified by the **Exchange**. *(Formerly rule 12.8)*

S842 Securities resulting from a **buying-in** transaction shall be delivered to the **liable party** as instructed by the **Exchange**. *(Formerly rule 12.9)*

S843 The **liable party** must ensure that securities received from the **Exchange** are immediately used to settle, in accordance with instructions received from the **Exchange**, the transaction to which the **buying-in** request is related. *(Formerly rule 12.10)*

Failure to buy-in (S850)

S850 Where the **Exchange** does not succeed in executing a trade pursuant to a **buying-in** request, the **Exchange** will notify the **requesting party**. Unless the **requesting party** then withdraws the **buying-in** request, the **Exchange** may, at its discretion, attempt **buying-in** on one more occasion only as follows:

S850.1 for transactions other than those dealt for guaranteed delivery, any time up to five days after the first attempt; or

S850.2 for transactions dealt for guaranteed delivery, on the next day following the first attempt. *(Formerly rule 12.11)*

Agreements to pass on costs (S860)

S860 Unless otherwise agreed in writing at the time of dealing, a buying **member firm** shall not pass on to a selling **member firm** the costs incurred by it as a result of its failure to deliver against another transaction, even though those costs may have been incurred because of that selling **member firm**'s failure to deliver. *(Formerly rule 12.12)*

Renounceable documents (S870)

S870 Transactions in renounceable documents are not subject to **buying-in**. However, where, because of non-delivery by the **liable party**, settlement of a transaction in a renounceable document is to be effected in registered form, a **buying-in** request may be submitted in respect of the registered security on the day after the settlement due date for the re-matched transaction or on a subsequent day. *(Formerly rule 12.13)*

Liabilities (S880-S881)

S880 Subject to rule S881, the **liable party** shall indemnify the **Exchange** against any and all liability in respect of any costs or losses sustained by the **Exchange** arising out of the execution of a **buying-in** request. *(Formerly rule 12.14(a))*

S881 A **member firm** that requests the **Exchange** to buy-in securities is responsible for any errors or omissions in its request and the **Exchange** shall not be liable in respect of any such errors or omissions. *(Formerly rule 12.14(b))*

Price and charges (S890-S892)

S890 In order to obtain delivery of the relevant securities to fulfil a **buying-in** request, the **Exchange** may execute a trade at a price higher than the current market price. The **liable party** shall pay the **Exchange** such price, regardless of the price of the original transaction that is the subject of the **buying-in** request. *(Formerly rule 12.15(a))*

S891 Any difference between the price paid to the **Exchange** and the price of the original transaction shall not be recoverable from, or payable to, the **requesting party** on settlement of the original transaction. *(Formerly rule 12.15(b))*

S892 The charges for **buying-in**, including ad valorem fines, administrative charges and other penalties, shall be published by the **Exchange** from time to time, together with the applicable collection arrangements. *(Formerly rule 12.15(c))*

Appendix D

Commodity Futures Modernization Act 2000

106TH CONGRESS

H. R. 5660

To reauthorize and amend the Commodity Exchange Act to promote legal certainty, enhance competition, and reduce systemic risk in markets for futures and over-the-counter derivatives, and for other purposes.

IN THE HOUSE OF REPRESENTATIVES DECEMBER 14, 2000
Mr. EWING (for himself, Mr. COMBEST, Mr. LEACH, Mr. LAFALCE, and Mr. BLILEY) introduced the following bill; which was referred to the Committee on Agriculture, and in addition to the Committees on Banking and Financial Services, Commerce, and the Judiciary, for a period to be subsequently determined by the Speaker, in each case for consideration of such provisions as fall within the jurisdiction of the committee concerned

A BILL

To reauthorize and amend the Commodity Exchange Act to promote legal certainty, enhance competition, and reduce systemic risk in markets for futures and over-the-counter derivatives, and for other purposes.

Be it enacted by the Senate and House of Representatives of the United States of America in Congress assembled,

SECTION 1. SHORT TITLE; TABLE OF CONTENTS.

(a) **SHORT TITLE.**–This Act may be cited as the

"Commodity Futures Modernization Act of 2000".

(b) **TABLE OF CONTENTS.**–The table of contents of this Act is as follows:

Commodity Futures Trading Commission website www.cftc.gov

Sec. 1. Short title; table of contents.
Sec. 2. Purposes.

TITLE I – COMMODITY FUTURES MODERNIZATION

Sec. 101. Definitions.
Sec. 102. Agreements, contracts, and transactions in foreign currency, government securities, and certain other commodities.
Sec. 103. Legal certainty for excluded derivative transactions.
Sec. 104. Excluded electronic trading facilities.
Sec. 105. Hybrid instruments; swap transactions.
Sec. 106. Transactions in exempt commodities.
Sec. 107. Application of commodity futures laws.
Sec. 108. Protection of the public interest.
Sec. 109. Prohibited transactions.
Sec. 110. Designation of boards of trade as contract markets.
Sec. 111. Derivatives transaction execution facilities.
Sec. 112. Derivatives clearing.
Sec. 113. Common provisions applicable to registered entities.
Sec. 114. Exempt boards of trade.
Sec. 115. Suspension or revocation of designation as contract market.
Sec. 116. Authorization of appropriations.
Sec. 117. Preemption.
Sec. 118. Predispute resolution agreements for institutional customers.
Sec. 119. Consideration of costs and benefits and antitrust laws.
Sec. 120. Contract enforcement between eligible counterparties.
Sec. 121. Special procedures to encourage and facilitate bona fide hedging by agricultural producers.
Sec. 122. Rule of construction.
Sec. 123. Technical and conforming amendments.
Sec. 124. Privacy.
Sec. 125. Report to Congress.
Sec. 126. International activities of the Commodity Futures Trading Commission.

TITLE II – COORDINATED REGULATION OF SECURITY FUTURES PRODUCTS

Subtitle A – Securities Law Amendments
Sec. 201. Definitions under the Securities Exchange Act of 1934.
Sec. 202. Regulatory relief for markets trading security futures products.
Sec. 203. Regulatory relief for intermediaries trading security futures products.
Sec. 204. Special provisions for interagency cooperation.
Sec. 205. Maintenance of market integrity for security futures products.
Sec. 206. Special provisions for the trading of security futures products.
Sec. 207. Clearance and settlement.

Sec. 208. Amendments relating to registration and disclosure issues under the Securities Act of 1933 and the Securities Exchange Act of 1934.
Sec. 209. Amendments to the Investment Company Act of 1940 and the Investment Advisers Act of 1940.
Sec. 210. Preemption of State laws.
Subtitle B – Amendments to the Commodity Exchange Act
Sec. 251. Jurisdiction of Securities and Exchange Commission; other provisions.
Sec. 252. Application of the Commodity Exchange Act to national securities exchanges and national securities associations that trade security futures.
Sec. 253. Notification of investigations and enforcement actions.

TITLE III – LEGAL CERTAINTY FOR SWAP AGREEMENTS

Sec. 301. Swap agreement.
Sec. 302. Amendments to the Securities Act of 1933.
Sec. 303. Amendments to the Securities Exchange Act of 1934.
Sec. 304. Savings provision.

TITLE IV – REGULATORY RESPONSIBILITY FOR BANK PRODUCTS

Sec. 401. Short title.
Sec. 402. Definitions.
Sec. 403. Exclusion of identified banking products commonly offered on or before December 5, 2000.
Sec. 404. Exclusion of certain identified banking products offered by banks after December 5, 2000.
Sec. 405. Exclusion of certain other identified banking products.
Sec. 406. Administration of the predominance test.
Sec. 407. Exclusion of covered swap agreements.
Sec. 408. Contract enforcement.

SEC. 2. PURPOSES.

The purposes of this Act are –

(1) to reauthorize the appropriation for the Commodity Futures Trading Commission;
(2) to streamline and eliminate unnecessary regulation for the commodity futures exchanges and other entities regulated under the Commodity Exchange Act;
(3) to transform the role of the Commodity Futures Trading Commission to oversight of the futures markets;
(4) to provide a statutory and regulatory framework for allowing the trading of futures on securities
(5) to clarify the jurisdiction of the Commodity Futures Trading Commission over certain retail foreign exchange transactions and bucket shops that may not be otherwise regulated;

(6) to promote innovation for futures and derivatives and to reduce systemic risk by enhancing legal certainty in the markets for certain futures and derivatives transactions;
(7) to reduce systemic risk and provide greater stability to markets during times of market disorder by allowing the clearing of transactions in over-the-counter derivatives through appropriately regulated clearing organizations; and
(8) to enhance the competitive position of United States financial institutions and financial markets.

From the operations teams point of view, the Act has implications in terms of the clearing organisation, risk reduction and client protection. **Section 207** covering clearing and settlement is important and so it is recommended that readers should study it to see what the implications are. It is also sensible to visit the CFTC and SEC websites for the latest updates on how CFMA is impacting.

It is important to remember that like all regulation to do with financial markets, the aims and objectives are the same as that of regulation in other jurisdictions but the way in which the regulation is enforced can vary significantly from that of other regulators and other jurisdictions.

Useful websites

www.aima.org	The Alternative Investment Management Association
www.fsa.go.jp	Financial Services Agency, Japan
www.fese.be	Federation of European Securities Exchanges
www.fsa.gov.uk	Financial Services Agency, UK
www.cftc.gov	Commodity Futures Trading Commission
www.sec.gov	Securities and Exchange Commission, USA
www.thelondonstockexchange.com	The London Stock Exchange, UK

Index

Access, 45
Additional voluntary contributions (AVCs), 5
Aggregated transaction, 57–8
Agreements, 104
Alternative Investment Management Association (AIMA), 99
Asia Pacific, 28–30
Audit, xiii, 47, 89–90
Austria, 23
Authorisation to market, 10–11
Automation, 42, 110

Bankruptcy, 45
Bare security interest arrangement, 16
Barings, x, xi-xii
Behaviour, 2–6
Belgium, 23
'Borrowing' assets, 83
Breaches of regulation, 89–104
Building Societies Commission (BSC), 8
Bundesanstalt für Finanzdienstleistungsaufsicht (BAFin), 21–2
Business leaders, xiii

Cancellation, 75
Capital Adequacy Directive (CAD), 16, 24, 41
'Chinese Walls', 3
Clearing houses, 11, 40
Client assets, 1–2, 13, 36–43, 53
Client money, 36–43
Collateral, 40–1
Commodity Futures Modernization Act (CFMA 2000), 26–7
Commodity Futures Trading Commission (CFTC), 17, 24, 26–8
Communication with clients, 12, 52
Compliance
  different markets, 21–33
  operations and, 35–49
  role, 17–19
Conduct, 2–6
Conduct of Business Rules, 12, 13–16
Confidence, 9
Conflicts of interest, 12, 52
Consumer protection, 7
Convertibility, 46
'Cooling-off period', 52, 75
Country Risk, 45
Credit Suisse First Boston, 31–2
Cross-border cash, money laundering, 64–5
Cross-border trading, 31–2
Custodians, 102
Custody, 13–14, 43–9
Customer Agreement, 60
Customers' interests, 12, 52
Cyprus, 23

Date of birth, 70
'Delivery versus payment transactions', 14–16
Denmark, 23
Derivatives
  money laundering, 63–4
  regulation, 96–7
  U.S. regulation, 27
  warnings, 10
Directors, xiii-xiv
Due diligence, 98–102

Electronic trading, 42, 110
Eligible custodians, 102
Eligible Securities Depository, 46
Enron, 81–2
European Economic Area (EEA), 17
European Economic Community (EEC), 16
European regulation, 16–17, 22–4
European Union Directives, 16
Exchanges, 11
Expropriation, 46

Federal Deposit Insurance Corp, 26, 27
Federal Reserve System, 26, 27
Final agreement, 44
Financial Action Task Force (FATF), 61
Financial crime, 7
Financial Services Agency (JFSA), 17, 28–30, 105–8
Financial Services and Markets Act 2000 (FSMA), 6
Financial Services Authority (FSA), ix-x, 6–7
  Conduct of Business Rules, 12, 13–16
  eligible custodian guidelines, 102
  objectives, 7
  Principles of Business, 12–13, 52–3
  roles and functions, 8–12
Finland, 23
France, 23
Fraud, 81–8
Free standing additional voluntary contributions (FSAVCs), 4–5
Friendly Societies Commission (FSC), 8
Fund management, 94–5
Fund managers, 2

Germany, 21–2, 23
Gilbert, Richard, 85
GLH (Derivatives) Limited, 84–6
Global markets, xiv, 16–17
"Golden hellos and goodbyes", 109
Government bonds, 10
Greece, 23
Griffin Trading Company, 83–6

'Hard sell', 52
Harmonisation, 110
Hawthorne Securities Limited, 86–7
Hedge funds, 9, 10–11, 53, 103
Home state, 22
Host state, 22
Hungary, 23

Iceland, 23
Identification evidence, 68–78
  certification of documents, 77
  joint applicants, 72
  new business for existing customers, 76
  records, 77–8
  when is it necessary?, 70–1
Incompetence, 5
Independent financial advisor (IFA), 5, 56
Independent intermediary, 56
Individual Savings Account (ISA), 53
Insider dealing, 81–8
Insurance Directorate (ID), 8
International Securities Market Association (ISMA), 42
International Securities Services Association (ISSA) recommendations, 97–8
Investment Management Regulatory Organisation (IMRO), 8

Investment Services Directive (ISD), 16, 22, 24
Investment trust, 53–6
Ireland, 23
Italy, 23

Japan, 17, 28–30, 105–8
Joint applicants, identification evidence, 72

Key features, 56
Know your customer, 68–78

Leaders of business, xiii
Lee, Darren, 84–5
Lloyds of London, 9
Loss, 46
Luxembourg, 23

Market confidence, 7
McLean, Malcolm, 3, 4
Mercury Asset Management, 2
Mis-pricing, 94
Misunderstanding, 5
Mitigating circumstances, 89
Money laundering, 47–8, 61–79
  assistance, 79
  cross-border cash, 64–5
  defined, 62
  derivatives, 63–4
  failure to report, 79
  penalties, 78–9
  Regulations (1993), 62–3
  Reporting Officers (MLRO) Annual Report, 66–8
  tipping off, 79
Morgan Grenfell, 32

National Crime Intelligence Service (NCIS), 74
Nationality, 70
Netherlands, 23
Norway, 23

Offer for sale, 11
Office of the Comptroller of the Currency, 26
Office of Thrift Supervision, 26, 27
Open-ended investment company (OEIC), 53–55
Operational functions, 110
Operational risk, 109
Operations
  breaches of regulations, 89–104
  compliance and, 35–49
  cross-border trading, 31–2
  practical issues, 17–19
Owners, xiii-xiv

'Packaged products', 53
Park, John Ho, 84
Pensions mis-selling, 3–6
Periodic statements, 59
Personal Investment Authority (PIA), 8
Personal pensions
  identification evidence, 73
  mis-selling, 3–6
Petty fraud, 81
Poland, 23
Polarisation, 56
Portugal, 23
Prime agreement, 44, 45
Principles of Business, 12–13, 52–3
Prospectus, 11
Protection of consumers, 7, 60
Public awareness, 7

Recommendations, 97–8
Record keeping, 57–60
Redemptions, 70–1
Registry of Friendly Societies (RFS), 8
Regulation, 1–19
  breaches, 89–104
  different markets, 21–33
  effectiveness, xi-xv
  future, 105–11
Regulator role, vii-viii, 51
Regulatory environment, 6–7

Reporting
to clients, 59
transactions, 41–3
Reputation, 91, 109–10
Request for proposal, 99–101
Residency, 70
Retail markets, 51–60
Right to use arrangement, 16
Rogue traders, xi, 83–6
Rose, Steven, 84
Rule 17(f)5 Questions, 45
Rule 17(f)7, 46

Safekeeping, 13–14
Scheme Particulars, 56, 104
Second Banking Co-ordination Directive (2BCD), 16
Securities and Exchange Commission (SEC), 17, 24, 25–6, 45
Securities and Futures Authority (SFA), 8
Service Level Agreement, 101, 102
Settlors, identification evidence, 73
"Single passport", 24
Slovenia, 24
Spain, 24
'Split caps', x
Spot checks, 47
"Spritzer", 109
Staff dealing rules, 82–3
Stock Exchange Electronic Trading System (SETS), 42
Stock lender, 103–4
Sub-Custody Agreement, 45
Suitability of products, 56–7
Supervision and Surveillance Division (S&S), 8
Supervisory Policy Statement on Investment Securities and End-User Derivatives Activities, 28
Surrenders, 70–1
Sweden, 24
Switzerland, 24
Szach, Scott, 84

Terms and Conditions, 57
Terms of Business, 60
Third parties, identification evidence, 73
Thorneywork, Neil, 86–7
Tied representative, 56
Tipping off, 79
Transaction reporting, 41–3
Trax, 42
Trust, 12, 52
Trust Financial Group (Europe) Ltd, 92–3
Trustees, identification evidence, 73
Trusts, identification evidence, 73

Unfortunate coincidences, 89
Unit trust, 53–55
United States, 17, 24–8, 45

Warrant and Derivatives Risk Warning, 56
Warrants and Derivatives Warning Notice, 10
WorldCom, 81–2